Introduction

The *Viceroy of India* was by no means either the largest or the fastest vessel built for the P&O Company but, without doubt, she remains the most luxurious ship ever owned by them. She was a 'one-off' vessel designed for an express service between London and Bombay—a lifeline—in those far off days of 'Empire'. She was also intended for exclusive 'yachting cruises', as this form of holiday was known in the 1920s and 1930s. Her cruises to the Norwegian Fjords and to Europe's Northern Capitals became legendary, and the 'society' pages of *The Times* frequently included names from her passenger lists.

Not only was her passenger accommodation unique, so also was her main propulsion machinery, at least in the British merchant fleet. She was equipped with turbo-electric machinery and so the headlines of the press reports in 1929 described her as: 'Britain's First Electric Liner'.

The loss of this fine ship in 1942 was a great blow to the P&O Company and, sadly, she became just one more casualty of war. Fortunately the loss of life was not great and help was at hand to pick up her crew members.

I hope this book can serve to remind readers of the 'golden' and leisurely age of sea travel, before 'plastic' international airports made one country much like any other and before the term 'jet lag' found its way into the English language. I hope also that the book will serve as a tribute to this great ship, which was P&O's first electric cruise liner.

Neil McCart
March 1993
Cheltenham

To: Caroline & Louise

Front and Back Covers: Paintings of the *Viceroy of India* which were used on the company's postcards during the 1930s. (Andres Hernandez Collection)

Inside Front Cover: The launch of the *Viceroy of India* which took place on Saturday 15 September 1928 at the Linthouse yard of Alexander Stephen & Sons. (P&O)

Inside Back Cover: The *Viceroy of India* alongside the P&O berth in Tilbury Docks. (The Museum of London)

Jacket Design: Louise McCart
© Neil McCart/FAN PUBLICATIONS
ISBN 0-9519538-1-8
1993

Typesetting & Printing by
The Starling Press Ltd
Rogerstone
Newport
Gwent NP1 9FQ

Famous l
SS VICE

—P&O's First Electric Cruise Liner

QUIS SEPARABIT

By Neil McCart

Contents

Published by FAN PUBLICATIONS
17 Wymans Lane Cheltenham GL51 9QA. 0242 580290

Chapter One

Steaming East—The Route To India

The origins of Britain's trade routes to India can be traced back to the final 25 years of the 16th century, when English and Dutch seafarers endeavoured to break the Portuguese monopoly of trade with Far Eastern countries. For Britain this task started in earnest in 1600 when the East India Company was incorporated as the 'Governor and Company of Merchants of London Trading into the East Indies'. The first English settlements on the subcontinent were at Surat just north of Bombay, and there followed 20 years of hostilities with the Portuguese until, in 1642, the British Governor of Surat and the Portuguese Viceroy of Goa came to an agreement whereby both countries could trade peacefully. The East India Company, with the permission of the local rulers, soon had three trading stations at Bombay, Calcutta and Madras. From these bases the company gradually gained control over a substantial part of India. In the first years of its existence, possibly only one or two vessels a year would be sent to India, but by the 18th century many more ships were sailing from the East India Docks in London bound for Bombay. They would return laden with tea, spices, silks and carpets. In 1784 the British government decided to exercise some control over the company and a Governor-General was appointed, a position which in 1855 became the Viceroy of India. The Viceroy was, in effect, the sovereign's representative, and Lord Mountbatten described the position as, '...the greatest office in the world.' However, although the Viceroy was the most powerful personage in Britain's Indian Empire, a ruler rather than a figurehead, he was held on a very tight rein by ministers and civil servants in London.

The first P&O vessels which were designed for service in Indian waters were the *Hindostan* and the *Bentinck* of 1842/43. They were wooden paddle-steamers of just over 2,000 gross tons with accommodation for 100 passengers. However, the mail contract for Bombay was still held by the East India Company and it was not won by P&O until 1853, after the East India Company lost a whole consignment of mail which was bound for the Indian port. Initially the contract called for a monthly service to Bombay, which, in the years before the Suez Canal was opened, entailed an overland journey between Alexandria and Suez. The desert sector of the journey was negotiated in a number of ways, including 'donkey chairs'—seats which were slung between two of these unfortunate animals.

The opening of the Suez Canal took away the need for this part of the journey, but the Bombay route still took second place to the Australian passage. By the last decade of the 19th century, Britain's foreign policy concentrated on what was considered to be the 'all important' route to India which, during Disraeli's administration became something of an obsession, with the Suez Canal becoming almost a British waterway. This policy had its effect on trade too and in 1908 P&O built a handsome 5,840-ton ship, the *SS Salsette*, to run an express service between Aden and Bombay. She would meet the weekly Australian steamer in Aden, where the passengers and mail bound for the Indian port would then tranship for a fast crossing of the Arabian Sea. With a speed of 20 knots the *Salsette* was the fastest ship in the P&O fleet, and this arrangement enabled the Australian vessels to omit the Bombay call and steam direct from Aden to Colombo.

Three years later, in October 1911, the new 'M' class liner *SS Medina* was fitted out as a Royal Yacht in order to convey King George V and Queen Mary to India for the Delhi Durbar. This royal tour ended at Portsmouth in February 1912 and after being refitted, the *Medina* was put onto the Australian route. At about the same time as the *Medina* joined the P&O fleet, the company decided to build a similar vessel for the London—Bombay mail service. For the first time in the company's history, the route to India was not taking a second place to the Australian service. The new ship was named *Kaisar i Hind*, a name which means 'Empress of India' and which was chosen in honour of the royal visit to the Indian Durbar. She was a vessel of 11,430 gross tons, and her accommodation was an improvement on all previous vessels; in particular her first class cabins, which were mainly single-berth, and the provision of an electric fan in each cabin,

The *Kaisar i Hind* was built in 1914 specifically for the London to Bombay mail service and, with a speed of 18½ knots, she was faster than any other P&O ship at that time.

P&O

The *Rawalpindi,* together with her sister ships, was designed by P&O for the Indian route. They were prestigious ships, but they would soon be eclipsed by the magnificent *Viceroy of India.*   *Harland & Wolff*

which resolved an old grievance of regular P&O passengers. In addition, the Smoking Room was more spacious and it extended through the entire width of the liner.

The *Kaisar i Hind* was a twin-screw ship powered by quadruple-expansion engines which developed 14,000 IHP and gave her a speed of 18½ knots, which was faster than any other P&O ship at that time. She was launched on Sunday 28 June 1914, but very little publicity was given to the event by the press, most newspapers being full of other sensational news. In the distant city of Sarajevo, Bosnia, the heir presumptive to the Austro-Hungarian Empire, Archduke Francis Ferdinand, and his consort had been assassinated on the same day that P&O's new ship took to the water. The *Kaisar* left Tilbury on her maiden voyage to Bombay on 24 October 1914. Sailing alone and unescorted, she set a new record for the voyage between Plymouth and Bombay of 17 days, 20 hours and 52 minutes. The vessel ran on P&O's reduced service to Bombay until October 1917, when she was taken up by the government under the Liner Requisition Scheme.

After the Armistice in November 1918 the *Kaisar i Hind* remained on government service and it was during 1920 that she was finally able to resume her London to Bombay service for P&O. This routine was interrupted briefly in 1921 when she was chartered to Cunard for one Atlantic crossing, and to the American Tourist Agency for a cruise to Scandinavia and other northern waters. Unfortunately the latter voyage was not a great success as the *Kaisar,* which had been designed for tropical waters, had no heating and in addition she was dogged throughout the voyage by thick fog.

Just before the outbreak of the First World War it had been decided that the P&O, and that other great shipping company, the British India S.N. Co, would merge. After the merger it was agreed that the aged chairman of P&O, Sir Thomas Sutherland GCMG, would retire and the chairman of the BI Line would take over as chairman of the amalgamated companies. It was during Lord Inchcape's 18-year tenure of office that P&O would lose the image which had been fostered by Kipling's 'Exiles' Line' of 1890:

'How runs the old indictment? ''Dear and Slow,''
So much and twice so much. We gird, but go.

For all the soul of our sad East is there,
Beneath the house-flag of the P&O.'

Lord Inchcape would introduce fast modern vessels and eventually he would ensure a whole new appearance for the company's ships.

In 1925 P&O introduced a successor to the *Salsette* which, sadly, had been lost during the First World War. The new vessel was the 10,602 gross ton *Razmak,* a handsome schooner-rigged vessel with two funnels and a counter stern. Her twin screws were driven by quadruple-expansion engines, with low-pressure, double-reduction geared turbines. This reliable machinery gave her a speed of 18 knots and she was able to carry 284 passengers, half of them being first class. Like the *Salsette,* she was intended for the Aden— Bombay shuttle service, and her maiden voyage to the Indian port started from Tilbury on 13 March 1925.

In fact the *Razmak's* five years of service with the P&O were spent mainly running between Marseilles and Bombay, and occasionally she would return to London. On her eastbound voyage she would embark 'overland' passengers at Marseilles and then make a fast passage to Bombay, calling only at Port Said and Aden. By January 1926 the four 'R' class ships, *Ranpura, Ranchi, Rawalpindi* and *Rajputana,* which had also been designed for the Indian route, were in service. These were prestigious ships, in which much of the internal décor was designed by Miss Elsie Mackay, the youngest daughter of Lord Inchcape. All four ships took their turn with cruising duties during the summer, which made the *Ranpura* and *Ranchi,* in particular, very popular ships.

The entry into service of the 'R' class ships marked the completion of the post-war building programme for P&O, and there was to be a lull of nearly four years before the next new vessels joined the fleet. However, during that time plans were afoot for the most imaginative and courageous step which the P&O Company had ever taken. Designs had been approved for a 19,700 gross ton ship with a speed of 19 knots, and with accommodation which, even today, is considered by many to be the most luxurious ever seen in a P&O ship. Primarily the new ship was built for the Indian mail service, but during her short career she would become famous for her luxury 'yachting cruises'.

Chapter Two

A Glasgow Launch

Saturday 15 September 1928 was a special day for the employees of the shipbuilding company Alexander Stephen & Sons and, indeed, for the city of Glasgow itself. The launch of a great liner there was always a great event, and particularly at the Linthouse shipyard of that family-owned company, which was one of the best known in the world. This was due to the wide range and diverse character of the ships built there and because of the company's reputation for work of the highest standard. They had constructed vessels for shipowners in every quarter of the globe, and these had included cruisers, destroyers, coastal steamers, yachts, cargo ships and ocean liners. It was the largest passenger liner ever built at the yard that caused such excitement on that September day. P&O had placed the order for the ship in March 1927, with the contract being signed at Glenapp, Lord Inchcape's family home. The original specification had called for a 17,000 SHP vessel powered by high-pressure, geared turbines, but this would be altered before the keel was laid. At 19,648 gross tons, with an overall

Lady Irwin with Lord Inchcape (left) and Mr F. J. Stephen at the launch of the P. & O. liner Viceroy of India at Glasgow on Saturday.

Noon on Saturday 15 September 1928 and Lady Irwin, the wife of the Viceroy of India, is about to send a bottle of wine crashing onto the bow of the new ship. She is accompanied on the launching platform by Lord Inchcape, the Chairman of P&O, and Mr F. J. Stephen of Alexander Stephen & Sons, the builders.

Author's collection

length of 612 ft, she was the largest and finest ship which had ever been built at Linthouse, and the most advanced technically. Originally P&O had intended to name the vessel *Taj Mahal,* after the white marble mausoleum at Agra by Shah Jehan, in memory of his favourite wife. However, this idea was dropped whilst the ship was on the stocks and the name *Viceroy of India* was substituted. It was very appropriate, therefore, that the launching ceremony for this fine new ship should be carried out by Dorothy, Lady Irwin, who was, at that time, the Vicereine and on a visit to the UK. Her husband, Lord Irwin, had become Viceroy of India in April 1926, at 45 years of age and he has been described as, '...the most Christian and the most gentlemanly of them all.' He remained in the office until April 1931, through some very turbulent years on the Indian political scene, although he is better remembered today as Lord Halifax, the Foreign Secretary to Chamberlain's government in 1939, when he supported the appeasement policy towards Hitler.*

The launching ceremony took place at noon, when Lady Irwin, accompanied on the launching platform by Lord Inchcape (who had just celebrated his 76th birthday), and Mr Frederic J. Stephen, the chairman of the shipbuilders, sent a bottle of wine crashing onto the *Viceroy's* bow. This in turn released the launching lever and the vessel thundered stern first down the slipway into the River Clyde. This was no mean feat, for the *Viceroy,* with an overall length of 612 ft, was the largest ship so far built by Alexander Stephen & Sons, and the Linthouse shipyard was at a particularly narrow section of the river close to the city centre and near where today's Moss Road joins the Clyde Tunnel. As the tugs pulled the *Viceroy* alongside the Shieldhall Wharf for fitting out, the guests at the launching ceremony were entertained to a luncheon. In his speech Lord Inchcape praised Alexander Stephen & Sons for delivering exactly on time, and he praised the skill and careful attention given to the ship by this family-run shipbuilding company.

Of course in those days the Clyde shipbuilders were 'second to none' and any delays were unthinkable. Lord Inchcape told his audience how he had attained his 'ideal' of a private cabin for each first saloon passenger and, although much work remained to be done, he was satisfied that the final delivery date of March 1929 would be met. He went on to say: 'I feel sure that the arrangements which have been planned, after much consideration, for the comfort of the 600 to 700 passengers will be appreciated. In setting these out, we had in view that, barring accidents, the vessel will be on service for the next five-and-twenty years, and even after that lapse of time she would not be considered out of date.' Had Lord Inchcape's prophecy on the vessel's career been realized, then the *Viceroy* would have been with us into the 1950s, but, then, in 1928, although Hitler had risen above the image of a 'street corner orator', he was still far from gaining power and it is doubtful whether, in the autumn of 1928, many people had even heard of him.

In proposing the toast of the new ship, Mr Frederic J. Stephen thanked Lady Irwin for the service she had performed in view of the fact that she had come a long distance at considerable inconvenience to perform the

*Edward Wood, 1st Earl of Halifax KG, OM, GCSI, GCIE, 1881-1959, Viceroy of India 1927-1931.

ceremony. After she had been presented with an inscribed glass bowl as a memento, Lady Irwin spoke of the thrilling interest she had found in performing the ceremony, and seeing the ship gliding so gracefully into the water.

For Lord Inchcape the launch of the *Viceroy* was a great achievement, but it must have been tinged with personal sadness, for much of the interior decoration had been designed by his youngest daughter Elsie Mackay, who had been lost in a flying accident earlier that year. She had accompanied Captain W. R. Hinchcliffe on an attempt at the 'long distance flight record' from Cranwell. Although he had sight in only one eye, Captain Hinchcliffe was an experienced pilot and there was great interest in his proposed flight. The press speculated about his partner on this occasion and Elsie Mackay's name was mentioned, but she denied that she would be accompanying Captain Hinchcliffe, stating that she had only, '...a small financial interest in the project.' In the event she proved to be the mystery passenger and the couple took off from Cranwell Aerodrome at 8.30am on 13 March 1928, in a Stinson-Detroiter monoplane *Endeavour*, which

Inchcape returned home immediately from Port Said in the *Razmak*, but there was little they could do for a widespread search failed to find anything. As a tribute to his daughter, Lord Inchcape ensured that a portrait photograph was placed on the mantelpiece in the *Viceroy's* first saloon Music Room.

1928 was, in fact, a year when pilots and their aircraft were beginning to make real progress and there were a number of record-breaking flights, one of which was a direct threat to the sea-borne trade between the UK and India. In February 1928 Captain Bert Hinkler flew from London to Australia in 16 days, and in April that year Captain Wilkins flew non-stop across the Arctic region. Two months later, in June, Captain Sir Charles Kingsford-Smith flew non-stop across the Pacific Ocean. As far as the *Viceroy of India* was concerned, the most significant flight that year took place only nine days before her launch. On the evening of 6 September 1928 Captain C. D. Barnard and Flying Officer E. H. Alliot alighted from their Fokker-Jupiter monoplane, *Princess Xenia*, at the conclusion of a four and a half day flight from India. Their object was, as they declared afterwards, '...to show the

The *Viceroy* is safely in the water and tugs prepare to tow her to the Shieldhall Wharf for fitting out. Note the debris from the slipway in the river. *Marine Publications International*

was fitted with a Wright-Whirlwind engine and enough fuel for 3,000 miles. As the aircraft headed west, it became clear that they were attempting a non-stop, transatlantic record-breaking flight. Three hours after taking off, at 11.30am, their aircraft was seen over County Waterford, Ireland, heading into heavy snowstorms with low visibility, and two hours later it passed Mizen Head. The last sighting of the aircraft was from a ship 170 miles off the Irish coast, as the *Endeavour* headed westward into even more severe weather. It is believed that they came down into the sea that same night, and no trace was ever found of bodies or wreckage.

At the time this happened Lord and Lady Inchcape were staying in Egypt and Elsie kept her part in the venture secret from her parents. They were not told until she had taken off from Cranwell, and Lord Inchcape kept the news of the missing aircraft from his wife for five days. It was said that Elsie had inherited much of her father's drive and personality and he had great pride and affection for her. Lord and Lady

possibility of establishing a fast passenger, mail and goods air service between Britain and India, and as an example of the rapid transport of merchandise by air we have brought as cargo, a large case of tea.' In Captain Barnard's words: 'We left Karachi at dawn on Sunday [2 Sept], and flew the same day to Bushire [Iran] on the Persian Gulf. In two stages on Monday and Tuesday [3 & 4 Sept] we crossed the desert at Aleppo [Syria] in Asia Minor, and on Wednesday [5 Sept] flew from there to Sofia. Today [6 Sept] we have flown non-stop for 1,400 miles from Sofia to Croydon.'

The launching of the *Viceroy of India* had coincided with a flurry of activity in the air, but it was to be some years before the Imperial Airways services had any effect on the routes once dominated by the great ocean liners, and on 15 September 1928, few, if any, of those attending the Glasgow launching ceremony would have taken these aerial exploits too seriously. That day belonged to the *Viceroy of India*.

This rare photograph, though not of particularly good quality, shows the *Viceroy* as she nears the end of her fitting out at Glasgow's Shieldhall Wharf.

Glasgow Herald

Chapter Three

Almost A Stately Home

Lord Inchcape's 'ideal' of a single-berth stateroom for every first class passenger was just one of the unique features of the *Viceroy's* accommodation. In addition, all the public rooms were in a period style with furnishings on a lavish scale. The colour schemes for the curtain and upholstery fabrics were mostly designed by Elsie Mackay, while the manufacturing and fitting was carried out by Waring & Gillow Ltd of Lancaster.

The *Viceroy* provided accommodation for 415 first class passengers in the midships section of the liner, on six decks from the Boat Deck down to E Deck. The public rooms were situated on A Deck, also called the Promenade Deck, which was directly beneath the Boat Deck. Right forward was the Music Room, a magnificent lounge, 60 ft long by 50 ft wide, in which the décor was an unusual blend of the early 18th century classical style and a distinctive contemporary theme. The bulkheads were panelled in hardwood and painted in pastel shades with what was described as 'quiet' gilding. The pilasters and pillars were decorated in rich bronze with a gold-dust effect. At the forward end of the room a handsome marble mantelpiece was surmounted by a brilliant cut mirror with a jade-green coloured border. Another feature of this room was a large central dome with a coloured glass laylight.

Large casement windows opened onto an enclosed observation gallery at the forward end of the Promenade Deck, which was protected all round by large sliding windows. The furniture included lounge settees, easy chairs and card-tables, while the floor was laid with parquet for dancing, and covered at other times with handmade English carpets which were specially designed for the room. There was also some individually designed wrought-iron work to both the glass screens and the bronze entrance doors, which opened aft into the first class entrance hall and main staircase. The main entrance halls on each deck were middle Georgian in style and panelled in English oak. The staircase itself was well planned, with large mirrors which enhanced the spacious appearance. On either side of the stairs there were two passenger lifts, each serving the first class dining saloon. The lift on the starboard side covered five decks, while the one on the port side travelled one deck more to open onto the upper pavement walk around the swimming-bath. On each deck the lift gates were of wrought iron decorated in green and flecked gold, with the cars themselves being panelled in walnut and oak, with silver and lacquer enrichments.

Immediately abaft the entrance foyer on A Deck on both

The first class Music Room, at the forward end of the Promenade Deck, was a magnificent lounge with an unusual scheme of decoration which blended classical styles of the early 18th century with a distinctive contemporary look. *Andres Hernandez Collection*

The first class foyer on A Deck. This view looks from port to starboard with the entrance to the Music Room at the left of the photograph, behind the palm which is in the foreground.
National Museums & Galleries on Merseyside

sides of the ship were corridor lounges leading to the Reading and Writing Room. These lounges were panelled in hardwood, enriched with soft green pillar casings and frieze ornamentation in gilt. The furniture included console tables and comfortable seating.

The Reading and Writing Room itself was a fine example of the Robert Adam style of decoration. Here too, the panelling was in hardwood, painted in pastel shades and the furniture was copied from some of the finest examples of the late 18th century period. The mantelpiece was based on an original at Kedlestone Hall, the seat of that notable Viceroy of India, Lord Curzon, and other details of the room were modelled on Harewood House. A large central dome, which formed the ceiling, housed several oil paintings and indirect lighting was concealed in four handsome Wedgwood vases.

The first class Smoking Room was situated towards the after end of A Deck and it was entered through vestibules at the top of a staircase from B Deck. The decoration was based on that of the stateroom in the Old Palace at Bromley-by-Bow, which had been built in the 1600s for James I. The original room is now preserved in the Victoria & Albert Museum at South Kensington. The panelling was in wire-brushed English oak with flat carving on the pilasters and frieze. The magnificent mantelpiece, also in oak, was richly carved with the royal coat of arms. This lofty room had a fine bracketed dome and a laylight in painted glass, with the

enriched plaster ceiling being copied from the original. A painting at the forward end depicted William Shakespeare arraigned before Sir Thomas Lucy for deer stealing, and two cabinets on either side of the painting were adapted from the Queen Anne of Denmark Press in Stirling Castle. Despite the 16th century design of the room, the furniture in it consisted of contemporary style lounge settees, easy chairs and card-tables.

Passing through wrought-iron gates on either side of the fireplace at the after end of the Smoking Room, passengers entered the Verandah Café. Here the bulkheads of stone and coloured tiles had been copied from an old Moorish palace and this effect was further enhanced by the richly decorated deckhead. The atmosphere of the Moorish sun-terrace was increased by the provision of comfortable cane furniture. On the Boat Deck, and separated from the promenade, was the first class children's playroom, which was described in a contemporary publication as, '...a large airy deckhouse specially designed for the purpose, with decorated walls and fitments suitable for children.'

The first class dining saloon, at the forward end of E Deck, was entered from the main staircase through a glazed vestibule. 392 passengers could be accommodated at one sitting in this elegant room. It was panelled in English walnut with gilt enrichments and pilasters in blue. Above the windows and doors were pastel decorations, while brilliant

The *Viceroy's* first saloon Reading & Writing Room was a fine example of pure Robert Adam decoration. The mantelpiece to the left of the photograph was based on an original at Kedleston Hall, the seat of that notable Viceroy of India, Lord Curzon. *Andres Hernandez Collection*

The first class Smoking Room was in the style of the stateroom of the Old Palace at Bromley-by-Bow, which had been built for James I in the 1600s. The enriched plaster ceiling was copied from the original which is actually preserved in the Victoria & Albert Museum. *Andres Hernandez Collection*

A close-up view of the magnificent mantelpiece in the first class Smoking Room. It was carved from oak and was richly embellished with the royal coat of arms. This view, looking aft, shows the wrought-iron gates leading to the Verandah Café.   *P&O*

The first class Verandah Café, where the decoration was copied from an old Moorish palace, with the effect further enhanced by the use of cane furniture.
Andres Hernandez Collection

The first class dining saloon at the forward end of E Deck was decorated in a contemporary style, and the brilliant cut mirrors, which can be seen round the hatch trunking, gave the room a more spacious appearance. *P&O*

The first class section of the Sports Deck looking forward along the port side promenade. In the centre the doors and windows of the Verandah Café can be seen.

Andres Hernandez Collection

The first class swimming-pool on G Deck in its magnificent Pompeian Hall with Roman pillars and marble floors. The pool itself was 24ft long and it was lined with softly coloured blue tiles.

Andres Hernandez Collection

The second class Smoking Room on B Deck was decorated in a 'Tyrolean' style.
Andres Hernandez Collection

The second class Music Room on C Deck was described as having a 'colonial' style of décor, with mahogany furniture. *P&O*

The second class Writing Room was a small compartment on the port side of C Deck, opposite to and forward of the Music Room.

Andres Hernandez Collection

cut mirrors on the sides of the hatch trunk created a more spacious effect throughout the saloon. The chairs were in English sycamore and walnut, with the coverings being reproductions of old needlework patterns. At the after end of the hatch trunking there was a handsome sideboard in walnut and gilt and the pillars were encased in blue marble, which added a pleasing note of colour to the apartment. The electric light fittings were in bronze with engraved glass panels, and the wall lights were held in carved alabaster bases. There were sliding casement windows which were fitted with jalousies to give fresh air and daylight to the room, and in the evenings electric lights were arranged behind them.

One of the distinctive features of the first class accommodation was the provision of a single-berth cabin for each passenger, on B, C or D Deck. Each stateroom was furnished with a polished oak bedstead, wardrobe and dressing-table, and a wash-basin with the added luxury, for those days, of running hot and cold water. There were also small cupboards, shelves, a chair and numerous hooks for hanging up clothes. Generally the furniture was in English oak and the floor was covered in heavy, parquetry-patterned linoleum. Sliding doors were fitted in order that families could join several rooms into one suite. On B Deck, 12 of the staterooms were fitted with private bathrooms and additional furniture, and on C Deck there were 20 de luxe cabins with private bathrooms and smaller adjoining rooms for passengers' maids or valets. These rooms were all

panelled in polished hardwoods, with unusual effects being obtained by the use of some very fine woods which had not often been seen in ship design. Again these rooms were fitted with communicating sliding doors, which allowed them to be used as double staterooms.

The final feature of the first class accommodation was the swimming-bath, which was situated on G Deck beneath the dining saloon. Access was gained by a separate stairway on D Deck or by the port side lift to the spectators' gallery, which gave a full view of the magnificent Pompeian hall with its Roman pillars and marble floors. The 24 ft long pool was lined with softly coloured blue tiles, and it was filled with sea-water which was heated to an agreeable temperature. Round the side of the pool there were changing cubicles and shower-rooms.

The 258 second class passengers were accommodated aft of the first class section, on five decks from A Deck down to E Deck. For the late 1920s and early 1930s, the conditions were excellent with well furnished and airy cabins, equipped with drawer and wardrobe space, and running water, which was something of a luxury on board ship in those days. Situated on D and E Decks, they were arranged on the 'Bibby' principle so that they were all 'outer' cabins with their own porthole. Most were two-berth rooms, but there were also three- and four-berth cabins available. The after section of A Deck was the second class sports area, with the Isolation Hospital right aft. The Smoking Room was on B Deck and here the decoration followed a Tyrolean theme, with walls in soft grey oak. The beam casings and the frieze to the panelling were picked out in bright colours, which were characteristic of the style, and the features of the room included a quaint chimney-piece with a niche for a clock, and a raised roof with colourfully painted plasterwork and a leaded laylight.

The other public rooms also were spacious and comfortable. The second class Music Room was on C Deck, situated directly beneath the Smoking Room. It was decorated in what P&O described as a 'colonial' style, with the bulkheads panelled in blistered poplar, and mahogany furniture. A note of black was introduced into the colour scheme with the pilasters and chimney-piece. The 'Queen Anne' style second class dining saloon was situated at the after end of E Deck and could seat 260 passengers at one sitting. This room was panelled in two shades of oak, with enrichments picked out in silver. The furniture was also in oak to match the bulkhead panelling and a selection of etchings in black and silver frames added interest to the walls.

Immediately forward of the staircase at the after end of C Deck, on either side of the No 5 cargo hatch trunking, there was a writing room and a children's playroom, and the open weather-decks at the after end of B and C Decks provided promenade spaces for the second class passengers.

The windows of the ship, at the sides of the Promenade space on A Deck and the public rooms, particularly in the first class section, deserve a particular mention. The covered promenade spaces on A and B Decks were of such a height that between each frame two windows were fitted, one above the other, with the upper fitting being fixed. There were 70 pairs of these windows on the two decks and they were fitted in heavy, cast-brass frames which were completely watertight when closed. In the first class Smoking Room and Verandah Café there were 26 sets of cast-brass casement-type, internally fastened windows with heraldic designs in coloured glass. These casement windows were bronze-finished inside with ornamental fastenings of Elizabethan design.

The master's accommodation was directly beneath the navigating bridge and chartroom, and the rest of the officers' cabins, together with the engineers' mess, were on the Boat Deck.

In a vessel which was designed for cruises to northern waters as well as voyages, via the Red Sea, to India, both heating and ventilation were most important and the *Viceroy's* system was, once again, quite unique. All the ship's ventilation was provided by the Thermotank Company of Glasgow, and it represented one of the most complete systems of mechanical ventilation ever installed on board a ship. The 'punkah louvre' system was used throughout the passenger and crew accommodation, and in the first class dining saloon there was a louvre over each chair.

All the 'punkah louvres' in the staterooms and cabin accommodation had a revolving arrangement fitted whereby they could be closed off, and in the public rooms the system provided for a complete renewal of air every three minutes.

Today the amounts of hardwood used in the construction of the vessel would be seen as environmentally unacceptable, but in the pre-war years of the late 1920s and early 1930s it was essential. In short, the occupants of any grand house in the British Isles would have felt completely at ease in the *Viceroy of India*, for she was almost a stately home herself.

A second class two-berth cabin showing its drawer and wardrobe space and, on the left, the wash-basin with 'running' water—not something to be taken for granted in those days.
Andres Hernandez Collection

Chapter Four

P&O's First Electric Liner

As well as the general interest which a new liner of this size always generated, it was the main propulsion machinery that made her one of the most remarkable vessels to be turned out from any British shipyard during the pre-war years. Apart from the *Moldavia* and *Mongolia* of 1922/23, the P&O Company had, since the *William Fawcett* of the 1830s, relied on steam reciprocating engines to propel its ships and so the choice of turbo-electric machinery, to drive twin propellers caused great excitement in the engineering and maritime world.

The man largely responsible for this choice was Mr R. T. Clarke, the P&O Superintendent Engineer, who made a thorough investigation of the various methods of propulsion available. Turbo-electric drive was not a new idea, and it had been used extensively in the United States of America. Mr Clarke's investigations had taken him to the USA and what had surprised him were the boundless possibilities for the use of electricity on board ship. He returned to the UK convinced that the electric motor was an ideal drive for marine propulsion. He had also considered the possibilities of diesel engines as the prime mover in connection with the electric drive, but he came down in favour of high-pressure, high-temperature, steam turbines. So the *Viceroy of India* was to be the first British passenger liner fitted with turbo-electric propulsion.

One of the drawbacks of this type of machinery was that it could not be constructed by the shipbuilders, and in this case the work was undertaken by the British Thomson-Houston Company Ltd of Rugby.* The main propelling machinery consisted of two turbo-alternators, both supplying current to two slow-speed synchronous motors, which were coupled directly to the twin propeller shafts. At reduced speeds only one alternator would be used to supply current to both motors, and by this means maximum fuel economy was obtained, both at full and reduced power. This was a great advantage in a vessel which was to spend a great deal of her time cruising at somewhat less than maximum speed and power. Four of the six water-tube boilers were able to

supply sufficient steam to run the one turbo-alternator at full power, thus ensuring good fuel economy at half power.

The two main turbo-alternators each developed 9,000kW at 2,700rpm and the turbines were of the Curtis impulse type with 18 stages, each having a Weir regenerative underslung condenser. The alternators were air-cooled, the air being forced in a closed circuit through the stator and rotor, and through a cooler which was situated immediately below the alternator frame. The temperature of the stator windings was indicated by two 12-point thermocouple outfits. The BT-H main propelling motors were of the synchronous three-phase type and they were situated at the after end of the engine-room, being coupled directly to the propeller shafts. Together the two motors developed 17,000 SHP at 109rpm, and like the alternators, they were air-cooled, with the air being forced through the motor windings and then through a cooler in a closed circuit by two independent motor-driven fans. Variation of propeller speeds in either direction was obtained by variation of the turbine speeds, whilst reversal of the propellers was attained by reversing the electrical connections of two of the three phases leading from the alternators to the motors by means of contactors, which were mechanically interlocked so that the operator could close them only in the correct sequence. This allowed the turbines to run continuously in one direction when manoeuvring, so that the total turbine capacity was available for steaming astern.

Each of the two BT-H motors was capable of continuously developing 8,500 SHP at 109rpm with the pressure of supply at 3,150 volts. Under full power each propelling motor was electrically connected to one turbo-alternator and was independent of the other motor and its turbo-alternator. However, at reduced powers, one turbo-alternator was used and it supplied current to both motors. Excitation current for the main alternators and motors was supplied from separate exciter sets taking direct current from the auxiliary turbo-generator sets. Immediately aft of the main propelling

*The company later became part of English Electric which is now owned by GEC-Marconi PLC.

A plan drawing which shows the layout of the *Viceroy's* machinery spaces.
Marine Publications International

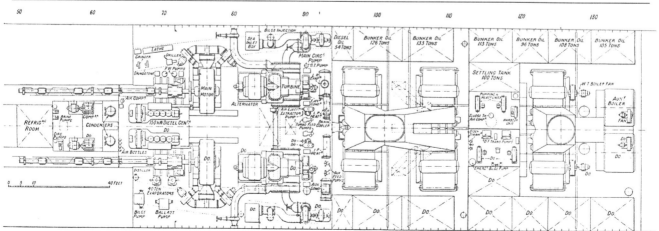

Elevation and Plan of Machinery Space of the "Viceroy of India."

The forward boiler-room in the *Viceroy of India*, showing the Yarrow and Scotch oil-fired boilers. *Marine Publications International*

motors were the thrust bearings, which were of the single-collar Michell type and fitted with Michell thrust meters.

The main feed-water circuit was of the closed type and with this system no feed-tank was fitted, the bottom of each main condenser forming a large reservoir instead. Distilled water-tanks were fitted in the vessel's double bottom to act as make-up tanks. The main condensers were of the Weir regenerative design which delivered their condensate air-free at vacuum temperature. The two main motor-driven centrifugal circulating pumps, which were supplied by W. H. Allen & Sons Ltd, each had a capacity, of 22,000 gallons per minute. The motor-driven water-extraction pumps withdrew from the reservoir in the main condenser base and delivered via the third stage coolers of the air ejectors, drain cooler and low-pressure heater, to the feed-pump suction. The feed-pump then delivered through intermediate- and high-pressure heaters to the feed-water regulators on the boilers. A low-pressure evaporator was fitted in the system in order to 'make up' the feed, with a capacity equivalent to 3% of the total feed-water. In addition there were two further high-pressure evaporators, each having a 40-ton capacity, and one distilling condenser of the same capacity.

Electric current for the separate exciters and the various motor-driven auxiliaries was provided by four BT-H direct-current 500kW turbo-generator sets, which were of the impulse type with single-reduction gearing. In port, current was supplied to the deck machinery by two 165kW diesel generators which were situated at the after end of the engine-room.

Steam for the main turbines was generated by six Yarrow oil-fired water-tube boilers, four of which were placed in

the after boiler-room and two in the forward boiler-room. In addition, two three-furnace, single-ended, oil-fired Scotch boilers were fitted in the forward boiler-room, for supplying steam at 230psi to the auxiliary turbo-generators. As the four boilers in the after boiler-room supplied sufficient steam when the *Viceroy* was travelling at speeds of up to 16½ knots, the two Yarrow boilers located in the after boiler-room could be shut down when only one turbo-alternator was required.

The six Yarrow boilers were each fitted with five oil burners and they supplied superheated steam to the main turbines at a working pressure of 375psi, and a temperature of 700°F.

For a ship which was to spend half of her time on the UK to India service, the question of cargo could not be ignored, and the *Viceroy of India* was provided with six cargo holds, each having a large steel hatch cover. The hatches were well provided with 19 derricks and 22 electric winches which could handle loads weighing between two and ten tons. In addition to considerable quantities of general cargo which could be carried, provision was made for 20,000 cu ft of refrigerated cargo, in two insulated spaces, with the refrigerating machinery being provided by J. & E. Hall Ltd.

The *Viceroy of India* was equipped with 13, 30-ft and two, 26-ft lifeboats and one 28-ft motor boat, with a total capacity of 1,155. This was ample provision for her maximum complement, when fully booked, of 1,093.

Without doubt the most unique feature of the *Viceroy of India* was her main propulsion machinery, which made her P&O's first electric liner.

The main turbo-alternators, contractor cubicle, and the main controls in the *Viceroy's* engine-room. *Marine Publications International*

The *Viceroy's* engine-room, looking aft from the boiler-room entrance. The main motors are to the left and right of the photograph and the diesel generators are further aft.

Laurence Sanderson

Chapter Five

The First Year

The New Year of 1929 saw the *Viceroy of India* still lying alongside the Shieldhall Wharf, just off Glasgow's Renfrew Road, with her fitting out almost completed. On the night of 8 January, in thick fog, the 7,100 gross ton steamer *Corinaldo*, which was inward-bound after a voyage from Canada, collided with P&O's new liner. The *Viceroy* sustained some damage to her starboard side amidships and the *Corinaldo* suffered damage to her bow. However, it was not serious and the small ship was able to berth at Princes Dock. The *Viceroy* herself was soon repaired and on 1 February she entered the Govan Dry Dock where the underwater hull was repainted. Her final two days in Glasgow were spent alongside the Yorkhill Quay on the north side of the river, and on 14 February 1929 she was ready to leave the shipyard and put to sea for her trials. She departed that morning for the journey down the River Clyde to Greenock, where she anchored off the Tail of the Bank. There then followed some four days of official trials on the Firth of Clyde, although her full-power trials could not be completed because of fog in the area. On Sunday 17 February, with four boilers and one turbo-alternator in use, a speed of 17.1 knots was realized on 97 rpm of the propellers and 10,410 SHP, which gave the vessel 'full marks' for economy. Unfortunately, after being weather-bound for several days, neither the consumption nor the full-power trials could be completed. However, this did not prevent a celebratory luncheon being held in the first class dining saloon, on Tuesday 19 February as the vessel lay at anchor off Greenock. Mr Alexander E. Stephen presided and he paid tribute to Miss Elsie Mackay, who had, '...specially approved

and augmented the decorative scheme', and 'whose desire it was that the new ship should be the last word in comfort and artistic harmony. Her object has been more than achieved, and it is a matter for deep regret that she was not spared to see the carrying out of her ideas.' He went on to pay tribute to the British Thomson-Houston Company who, '...have been a revelation of thoroughness and efficiency, and they have spared no efforts and expense to make the vessel a success. There has been not one indication of trouble with the running of the turbines or electrical gearing.'

After spending another week at anchor off Greenock with thick fog preventing completion of her trials, the *Viceroy* was finally able to continue her runs on the measured mile. The extensive programme of trials was finally completed successfully on the evening of Monday 4 March 1929 and the *Viceroy* went to anchor once again off the Tail of the Bank. Unfortunately, apart from delays owing to weather conditions, what had been a very successful series of trials was marred by a fatal accident in the final hour. As the vessel was anchoring, a pin came out of one of the shackles on the anchor chain and flew across the foredeck, striking and killing Mr Alexander Monro, a Lloyd's Registered Surveyor. The *Viceroy* remained at anchor for two days following the accident, while divers went down to recover the anchor and cable which had been lost, but this did not prevent the ship being handed over to the P&O Company.

The *Viceroy's* first master was Captain Basil James Ohlson DSO, RD*, RNR. He was born in Hull on 29 November 1873, his father being the Dean of Rotherham and the Headmaster

The *Viceroy* ran her trials between 17 February and 4 March 1929, and they were hampered by thick fog. Here she is seen at speed in the Firth of Clyde on a misty day.
University of Glasgow

Although the trials were completely successful, they were marred by a tragic accident in which a Lloyd's Surveyor was killed. In this view the *Viceroy* is at anchor off Greenock.

University of Glasgow

of Rotherham Grammar School. There was a strong tradition in the family that the elder son should enter the Church, but this was not at all to his liking, and so despite the protests of his father, he joined the prominent shipowners Devitt & Moore, in 1892 as an Apprentice. His first ship was the *Derwent*, a handsome barque built in 1867. Devitt & Moore carried up to 40 Apprentice Boys in their cargo-carrying ships and they received a sound training in navigation and related subjects. Life aboard the 19th century sailing ships was hard and dangerous, and the apprentices had to 'turn-out' and climb the rigging alongside the crew members to raise and trim the sails above heaving seas. His second ship was the clipper *Rodney*, which also carried up to 60 passengers in comparative comfort.

In 1896, 23-year-old Basil Ohlson left Devitt & Moore to join the P&O Company as Fifth Officer, his first appointment being to the 4,759 gross ton *Parramatta*. In July 1905, whilst serving as the Second Officer of the *Macedonia*, he married, and then in 1913 he gaind his Master's Certificate. During the First World War he was engaged in intelligence work and he was awarded the DSO for service in Mesopotamia (now Iraq). In 1918/19 he was stationed at Archangel, where he received Imperial Russia's equivalent of a knighthood, the Companion of the Order of St Vladimir. In 1919, upon his return to the P&O Company, he was appointed as master of the company's troop transport *Himalaya*. Subsequently he commanded the *Baradine*, *Balranald*, *Moldavia*, *Macedonia*, *Assaye*, *Oceana*, *Mongolia*, *Ranchi* and *Maloja*,

before being appointed to the *Viceroy of India* in the early days of 1929.

Following repairs to her anchor chain, the *Viceroy* left Greenock on Thursday 7 March 1929 for her voyage to London. At noon the next day she rounded The Lizard and set course for the Straits of Dover, arriving off Gravesend early in the morning of Saturday 9 March, and by midmorning the new ship was alongside No 31 berth in Tilbury Docks.

Despite the fact that in almost every year since 1918 Tilbury had seen some new addition to the fleets of fine ships which sailed worldwide from the River Thames, there had been nothing as luxurious or as revolutionary as the *Viceroy of India*. Painted in traditional P&O colours at that time, black hull, light brown upperworks and black funnels, she was the centre of attention. There is no doubt that her design, with a slightly raked stem, cruiser stern, two tall masts and two elliptical funnels, which were raked aft, gave an excellent balance, and this was further enhanced by her lofty superstructure. During the two and a half weeks in which she lay alongside at Tilbury, there was a steady stream of shipping correspondents from the newspapers and journals visiting the *Viceroy*, all of whom wrote at length and with undisguised admiration of the luxurious accommodation on board.

On Thursday 28 March 1929, with a full passenger list, the *Viceroy* left Tilbury for the maiden voyage to Bombay. With her breadth of 78 ft, great care was needed to

On Thursday 28 March 1929, with a full passenger list, the *Viceroy* leaves Tilbury Docks for her maiden voyage to Bombay.

Author's Collection

manoeuvre her through the old lock gates (situated on the south side of the docks) and into the tidal basin. The lock itself was 79ft 6 in wide, and considerable time and skill was required to get her safely through without damaging either the vessel or the lock walls. A number of Lascars from other P&O ships were at the quayside to help with the moving of heavy hawsers and the working of the ship as she passed through with only nine inches to spare on either side of the ship. Amongst the VIPs on board for the voyage was Sir Malcolm Hailey, the Governor of the United Provinces. Although she was fully booked, only 75 passengers were making the complete voyage to Bombay. Her route, which was to become very familiar over the ten years of her peacetime service, was via Gibraltar, where she remained only a few hours, then Marseilles, which was often a 24-hour stop. Here she would embark the overland mails and passengers who arrived on the 'Bombay Express' from London. They had usually left London about 24 hours before, which saved them three or four days' travelling and, more importantly for some, avoided the passage across the Bay of Biscay. After leaving Marseilles on 6 April, she called at Malta two days later and on 10/11 April she made her first southbound transit of the Suez Canal. Three days after leaving Suez she rounded Perim Island and a few hours later she was moored to a buoy off Steamer Point in Aden. During the afternoon of Sunday 14 April, after a stay of only a few hours, she left the port for a four-day voyage across the Arabian Sea to Bombay. At 6am on Friday 19 April 1929, three weeks after leaving Tilbury, she anchored in mid-stream off Bombay Harbour. Later that morning she went alongside No 2 berth of Alexandra Dock, ahead of the company's 'R' class vessel, *SS Rawalpindi*. After a stay of two weeks in the Indian port, during which time the *Times of India* devoted many pages to descriptions of the new liner, on Saturday 4 May the *Viceroy* moved round to Ballard Pier where she embarked her passengers during the afternoon. Amongst the many VIPs in the first class accommodation were H.H. The Maharaja of Alwer and Lady Montague Butler, the mother of a future government minister, 'Rab' Butler. Sadly, that same day there was widespread fighting in the city between Hindus and Muslims during which British troops had to maintain order. Even so, by the evening, as the *Viceroy of India* left Ballard Pier, there were 60 dead and 160 injured. The *Viceroy's* return voyage took her to the same ports that were visited on the outward journey, with an additional short call at Plymouth, where she anchored just long enough for a tender to collect the mails. She arrived back in Tilbury Docks on completion of her maiden voyage on Friday 24 May, having been away for eight weeks. On the following day the P&O, and the *Viceroy of India*, played host to members of the Postal Union Congress, although on her maiden voyage she had broken no records and the mails had not arrived at their destinations any quicker than before.

For the next three months, during the summer of 1929, she made five cruises, all of which took her into the Mediterranean, and most of her itineraries would be very familiar to P&O cruise passengers today. As with all her 'yachting cruises', as they were described in those days, the *Viceroy* carried first class passengers only and they could enjoy the facilities of the first and second class public rooms. P&O had planned a programme of 15 cruises that summer and these were undertaken by the *Viceroy* and the 'R' class vessel, *Ranchi*. The *Viceroy* left London for her first cruise, a two-week voyage to Malaga, Alicante, Barcelona, Palma, Philippville (now Skikda in Algeria), Gibraltar and Vigo, returning to Southampton on Friday 14 June. Her next two cruises started and terminated at Southampton and amongst the ports visited were Arosa Bay, just north of Vigo in Spain, Oran and Tangier. Her final cruise for the summer of 1929 was a 28-day sojourn in the Mediterranean, making 14 ports of call including Cagliari, Naples, Messina, Kotor, Split, Venice and Dubrovnik. She made an overnight call at Venice and when she left on the afternoon of Friday 9 August, she rammed the local tug *Olando,* which had to be beached in order to prevent it sinking. Fortunately no one was hurt and the *Viceroy* was able to continue the cruise which took her to Rhodes and Malta, before returning to Tilbury Docks on the morning of 23 August.

She sailed again the same day, bound once more for Bombay, and fortunately it was the last time she would have to negotiate Tilbury's narrow entrance lock for, in September 1929 the new, wider lock on the western side of the docks was opened.

Speaking at P&O's annual general meeting on 30 August 1929 Lord Inchcape had this to say about the *Viceroy of India:* 'The ship has so far made two voyages to Bombay and back and five pleasure cruises. Her accommodation, fuel consumption, speed and sea-going qualities have quite come up to what was expected and reflect the greatest credit on our Naval Architect, our Superintending Engineer, our Nautical Advisers, our Superintending Pursers and the builders, Messrs Alexander Stephen & Sons. So far the *Viceroy of India* has carried 5,800 passengers, and we have had dozens of letters of appreciation of the ship and of all on board from Captain Ohlson downwards.' Another speaker at the meeting paid tribute to the steadiness of the ship which had encountered a mistral in the Mediterranean while he was on board. He also spoke of the absence of 'beat' which was so noticeable in ships with reciprocating engines and, after congratulating the chairman, he went on to say how much he hoped that they would build more like her. In fact Lord Inchcape did have plans to do so, but by the end of 1929 recession had taken a grip on western economies.

After arriving back in London in late October, the *Viceroy* sailed for Bombay again on 8 November. On the return voyage she departed Port Said at 11.57pm on 22 December bound, initially, for Malta. At 6.15am the next morning she received an SOS message from the small Italian steamer, *Maria Luisa,* which was *en route* from a Red Sea port to Trieste. The Italian ship, whose position was Lat 32°-32'N/Long

The *Viceroy* leaving the Thames and heading into a choppy sea.

P&O

30°-05′E, reported that she was taking in water, but when the *Viceroy* acknowledged the signal she received the following reply: 'Not necessary to abandon immediately, continue your voyage.' However, just over three hours later, she received a further SOS from the *Maria Luisa* stating: 'Taking water through No 1 hatch and sinking, save crew.' Captain Erasmus J. Thornton, who had relieved Captain Ohlson on 4 November, immediately altered the *Viceroy's* course, and with the stricken ship only 30 miles away, she arrived off the *Maria Luisa* at 11.19am. The Italian vessel was lying very low in the water with her forward decks awash. Despite the severe squall which was blowing at the time, the *Viceroy's* two motor lifeboats were able to rescue the Italian ship's master and his 24 crew members. After ensuring that navigation warnings were sent out, Captain Thornton continued his voyage and, at 3.30pm on Christmas Day, upon their arrival at Malta, the crew of the *Maria Luisa* were entrusted to the Italian Consul. It was fortunate that the *Viceroy* had been so close, for shortly afterwards, a salvage tug which went to the scene was unable to find any trace of the wreck. The *Viceroy* then resumed her voyage and arrived safely back in London on 3 January 1930.

After a short refit and maintenance period, the *Viceroy* sailed for Bombay once again on 17 January 1930, arriving in the port three weeks later on 7 February. It was during her two-week stay there, while she was lying as usual at No 2 berth Alexandra Dock, that she was involved in a collision through no fault of her own. The 6,066 gross ton BI steamer *Warfield** was being towed to an adjoining berth when she struck the *Viceroy's* port quarter with her stern, causing some slight damage at the point of impact. The force of the collision, however, forced the *Viceroy* against the fenders which were designed to keep her off the quay wall and she suffered some minor damage above the water-line, to the starboard side amidships. Her superstructure, which was forced down towards the quayside on the starboard side, struck a crane and bent it over to quite a crazy angle. Fortunately for the ship, it was the crane that gave way and not the *Viceroy's* superstructure, and so the damage to the liner was only slight. During the next four days repairs were carried out and she sailed, on schedule, for London at 2.30pm on Saturday 22 February 1930. Amongst the distinguished passengers on board were Lord Hailsham (the father of the present title holder), the Earl of Rosse and H. E. Sultan Sir Abdul Karim. The voyage home passed without incident and followed the usual route via Aden, Suez, Malta and Marseilles, with additional calls at Monaco and Algiers. She arrived back in Tilbury Docks on 14 March, just over 12 months since she had first arrived in the port from Glasgow. Although no attempts to break any speed records between Europe and India had been made, the *Viceroy's* first year of service, both cruising and on the mail run, had been a success.

*The *Warfield* was eventually bombed by aircraft and sunk off the coast of Portugal on 15 August 1943, therefore outlasting the *Viceroy of India* by nine months.

Chapter Six

The Voyage To India

Soon after the *Viceroy of India* arrived in London from Bombay on 23 May 1930, Lord Inchcape held a dinner on board, which was attended by Prince Arthur of Connaught, one of the two surviving children of Queen Victoria, and many other distinguished guests. One elderly gentleman lamented the disappearance of the 'cuddy' in these 'new' steamships, although he praised the *Viceroy* and the P&O Company as being, '...the real descendents of, and a link with old "John Company".' However, Britain's relationship with India was fast changing and one passenger on the *Viceroy's* last Indian voyage, Sir Penderal Moon OBE, who was, at that time, an Indian Civil Service recruit, recalls: 'Leaving England was really worse than going back to school. Amongst the many topics we discussed on the voyage out was how long the Raj was going to last and the general consensus was, "Well at any rate it'll last about 25 years which will entitle us to proportionate pensions." We were fully conscious that we were on a sinking ship, as it were.' Sir Penderal recalled how, on the voyage, social classes were quick to establish themselves on board and how, 'One was thought rather badly of if you didn't support the P&O—the British line.' The social divisions to which he referred were usually along these lines; the military, ICS and government, planters, families travelling to join husbands and fathers and, last of all, the missionaries. Sir Penderal recalls of his voyage in the *Viceroy* that the protocol from life ashore was carried on aboard ship and, 'If you saw a major or a colonel in front of you, you naturally stepped aside to let him pass, and if you were late coming back when we called at various ports

you were sent for by the captain and asked why you hadn't come back when you heard the ship's siren going.'

However, at the end of May 1930, the *Viceroy* took on different types of passenger as she began her summer season of six cruises. The first four were two-week cruises to the Mediterranean for which she used Southampton as her terminal port. She sailed at 2.15pm on 26 July 1930 for the fifth cruise, which was a two-week voyage round the British Isles. After calling at Falmouth, Milford Haven and Douglas, Isle of Man, she made an overnight stop at Bangor in Northern Ireland before calling at Lamlash and Oban. From there she steamed north again to Stornoway on the Isle of Lewis, before sailing east through the Pentland Firth and into the North Sea, calling then at Invergordon in the Cromarty Firth. Her final port of call, on 6 August, was Aberdeen where she spent a day before returning to Tilbury on 8 August. The final cruise of 1930 took her north again, this time to the Norwegian Fjords and to Iceland, cruises for which she was to become renowned. On 11 August 1930 she arrived in Lerwick, Shetland Isles, where a Viking pageant of welcome was staged by the town's citizens. It took the form of a small play performed on the water, and as the liner arrived at her anchorage she was approached by a replica Viking ship, manned by 'traditional Norsemen' in Viking dress, complete with axes, shields, coats of mail and winged helmets. Once at anchor the Viking ship was joined by another crewed by Shetland girls in traditional costume. After climbing the accommodation ladder, both 'warriors' and 'lassies' were welcomed on board by Captain Ohlson. The visitors were

The *Viceroy* at anchor off Steamer Point in Aden. Note the awnings on the first class Sports Deck to protect passengers from the searing heat.
P&O

introduced by a local dignitary, who greeted the passengers in this fashion: 'Commander Ohlson, and all you good people of the *Viceroy of India*, Skol! We welcome you to the North Land. We welcome you to Ultima Thule.' For then, just as today, the people of Shetland were proud of their Norse descent. Captain Ohlson did not forget either, that his fine new ship, the pride of the P&O fleet, was anchored close to the House of Gremista where Arthur Anderson, a founder of the P&O nearly 100 years previously, had been born. Once penniless, he had become chairman of the great P&O

Captain W. P. Townshend now took command of the *Viceroy* and the vessel's next voyage to India commenced on Friday 7 November 1930. All went well until noon on Thursday 27 November, the day before she arrived in Bombay, when she lost a blade from her starboard propeller. On the return voyage she called at Gibraltar on 29 December 1930, and on Wednesday 31 December at 4.15am, whilst crossing the Bay of Biscay, she received this SOS message from the Greek ship, *SS Theodoros Bulgaris*: 'In position 45°-30′N/7°-28′W. Ship sinking. Save crew.' Captain

At the end of an outward voyage, the *Viceroy* approaches Bombay. Again she has sun canopies out on the first class Sports Deck and over the crew's forecastle space.
P&O

Company and the MP for Orkney & Shetland. After spending the day anchored off the town, the *Viceroy* left Lerwick that evening for Reykjavik, capital of Iceland, and from there she steamed across to the Norwegian Fjords where she sailed up the Sognefjord to Laerdal, then on to Bergen and Tysse.

It was the end of August 1930 when the *Viceroy* made her first autumn sailing of the year to Bombay, returning on 24 October once again to Tilbury. It was Captain Ohlson's last voyage with the *Viceroy* for, after finishing his leave, he went north to Barrow-in-Furness to 'stand by' the new P&O liner, *Strathnaver*, which was being built by Vickers Armstrong.

Townshend altered course immediately and the *Viceroy* made a 30-mile dash in heavy seas to assist the stricken vessel.

It was the second time in three months that the Greek ship had been in trouble, the previous occasion being on 20 September 1930, again in the Bay of Biscay, when her steering gear had failed and her cargo of grain had shifted. In the event, the *SS British Advocate* rescued her crew and the German vessel *Livadia* found the abandoned Greek steamer 120 miles south-west of Ushant and towed her to Brest. After undergoing repairs, the *Theodoros Bulgaris* returned to the Black Sea where she loaded another cargo of grain at

Constanza, Romania, and sailed from that port for Hamburg on 12 December 1930, the day before the *Viceroy* left Bombay for her voyage home.

At 12.25pm on 31 December, with a severe gale blowing and in heavy seas, the *Viceroy of India* arrived at the scene with the sinking ship right ahead and flying the signal FJ, 'send lifeboat to save crew.' It was an hour before Captain Townshend was able to manoeuvre the *Viceroy* into a position here he felt able to stop and send away the port accident boat, commanded by the Third Mate, Mr C. S. Cooke. Two hours later, at 3.25pm, the boat returned with 17 crew members and two stowaways, and towing the stricken ship's own lifeboat which carried the master and the remaining 11 crew members. At that time the *Theodoros Bulgaris* had a list of 40° to starboard and, after sending out navigation warnings, Captain Townshend left the scene to resume the voyage to Plymouth, where the *Viceroy* arrived at 9am the next morning for a brief call. This time the *Theodoros Bulgaris* was not seen again, and it must be assumed that she sank soon afterwards. The story later had a happy sequel, for in August 1932 silver medals and diplomas were received from the Greek government for Captain Townshend, Mr W. E. L. S. Pocock, the Chief Officer, and Mr C. S. Cooke, the Third Officer, as well as seven Quartermasters who had manned the *Viceroy's* accident boat. The rescue had been extremely hazardous as they could not approach too close to the *Theodoros Bulgaris* as the

heavy seas were likely to swamp them, and there was the possibility of the steamer's overhanging gear fouling the boat. In the event they threw ropes to the crew and dragged them, one by one, through the sea. The remainder, whilst they were waiting to be rescued, managed to launch their own boat and this was taken in tow. The *Viceroy's* crew members had acted very bravely and fully deserved the awards.

During the early part of 1931 the *Viceroy* made two voyages to Bombay and on her return journey an additional call at Monte Carlo was included. In mid-May she started her summer season of eight cruises from London and Southampton, and in those days the first class fare for a 13-day cruise started at 24 guineas (£25.20). In July and August that year she repeated her cruises to northern waters, and towards the end of September she left once more for India. Just a few weeks later the brand new passenger ship *Strathnaver*, the first of the 'White Sisters', joined the fleet and so the *Viceroy* was no longer the newest of the company's ships. Although she was not involved in any major incidents during these voyages there were often 'mini-dramas' on board. During her homeward voyage in December 1931, while at Aden, she embarked a stowaway from the P&O liner *SS Chitral* which was outward-bound to Australia. This young Frenchman had stowed away in Marseilles, hoping for a voyage to the antipodes, but he had been discovered and landed at Port Said. He was obviously a determined individual for he managed to escape from

Homeward-bound, the *Viceroy* is seen here anchored off Gibraltar.

P&O

Under way on the Thames, a fine port quarter view of the *Viceroy of India*. *P&O*

The *Viceroy* at anchor off Funchal, Madeira, on 25 August 1932. Note the 'bum-boats' clustered round the after end of C Deck, selling their wares to passengers.
E. H. Cole

An advertisement for the *Viceroy's* cruise to the West Indies in December 1932. *Author's Collection*

during the vessel's northbound transit of the Suez Canal, he was exercising on the forward well-deck when he leapt from the ship and landed on the west bank of the canal where he disappeared among the sand dunes. Eight days later, a second class passenger who had spent over ten years in India, died from a serious illness, within 72 hours of home. Today, when one reads the bridge logs of the *Viceroy of India*, some of these sad dramas sound almost like passages from a Somerset Maugham novel, as in: '27 April 1932, 9.45am, position Lat 45°·15′N/Long 8°·00′W. Mr R. S. Ardill, Supernumerary Fourth Engineer, was reported missing by the Chief Engineer. At 4.50am on 27 April 1932 Assistant Engineer J. Saunders saw him in his cabin when he complained of pains in the back of his head. The messroom boy saw him at 5.30am dressed in a bath towel. His uniform suit was missing and it is presumed he dressed before leaving his cabin. Presumed lost overboard.' Another entry in the 1930s reads: 'At about 7am J. Anderson, Cabin Steward, went into cabin 47 with morning tea for Mr T. W. Dearlove, first saloon passenger. He found the cabin vacant, bed tumbled and saturated with blood. He reported the matter and the ship was searched but without result. On a further search being made of the cabin, a blood-stained safety razor blade was found on a shelf over the bed, and a note on the dressing table saying ''I can't sleep and it is driving me mad. Please send my things to the enclosed address.'' Mr Dearlove was last seen at 11.50pm when he left the Smoking Room where he had been playing bridge. It is assumed that Mr Dearlove was lost overboard.' These were just two sad incidents among many that illustrate the individual human tragedies which were all part of the 'burden of Empire'.

On Saturday 17 September 1932, on completion of her summer cruise programme, the *Viceroy* left the Tilbury Landing Stage, which had been recently opened by the Prime Minister, Mr Ramsay MacDonald, for another voyage to Bombay. With Captain E. J. Thornton RNR in command, this was to be the first of her 'express' sailings to and from the Indian port calling only at Marseilles and Port Said. She actually completed the journey to Bombay in 17 days, one hour and 42 minutes, which was 19 hours less than the previous record time which had been set by the P&O vessel *SS China* in 1919. During the voyage the *Viceroy's* average speed was 17.85 knots and copies of *The Times* newspaper of 20 September 1932, which had been taken on board at Marseilles, reached the reading rooms of the clubs in Simla on Wednesday 5 October, just 15 days later. The round voyage ended at Tilbury on the morning of Wednesday 26 October 1932, after just five and a half weeks away. Following one more express voyage to India she sailed from London on 21 December 1932 for a most unusual cruise, which was advertised as 'A Christmas Cruise to the West Indies by P&O'. Amongst the passengers on this occasion was Sir A. Edward Aspinall, a wealthy businessman with extensive commercial interests in the West Indies. He had also written guide books about the islands and whilst on board he delivered a series of talks to his fellow passengers, one imagines in the manner of today's port lecturer. The 38-day cruise took the ship to several exotic ports, including Bermuda, Kingston (Jamaica), Antigua, Grenada, Barbados, Madeira and Casablanca. It proved a great success and so it was repeated in future years. By the end of 1932 both the *Strathnaver* and the *Strathaird* had entered service with the P&O, both of them on the Australian mail service and cruising routes. However, for many people the *Viceroy of India* still remaind the company's most luxurious vessel and berths on her voyages and cruises were always in great demand.

police custody and get back on board the *Chitral*. However, having been found a second time, he was put on to the *Viceroy* for the journey back to Marseilles. Four days later,

Chapter Seven

A Royal Occasion And Another Rescue

In August 1933, only one month after Adolf Hitler's Nazi party was declared to be the only legal political party within Germany, the *Viceroy of India* undertook her first visit to that country when she made a southbound transit of the Kiel Canal and called at Hamburg for a day. At the end of that year, following the success of her 1932 West Indies cruise, she made another winter cruise to the Caribbean, which included the South American ports of Bahia (now Salvador) and Rio de Janeiro in Brazil. She left Gravesend on Friday 29 December 1933, bound for the Channel, after which she set southerly courses to Madeira and the Cape Verde Islands so that after only two days out she reached warmer climes. Many of the passengers had reserved their cabins 18 months in advance of the voyage. On the evening before she sailed for the cruise, Mr F. H. Grosvener, the manager of P&O's Passage Department, and the *Viceroy's* relief master, Captain J. W. Hartley, hosted a dinner on board. They drew attention to the speed of the vessel's 'turn-round' at Tilbury which, on occasions, meant that the ship sailed again within 48 hours of her arrival. Another point of interest was that during the summer cruising season the company had five ships employed on 27 cruises, during which they carried 21,000 passengers. 'P&O Cruises' was as much an institution 60 years ago as it is today. The Postmaster General also voiced his approval of the

service by announcing that express correspondence for India, 'should be superscribed, "By *Viceroy of India*".'

The *Viceroy* arrived back in Tilbury in mid-February 1934 and there followed another year of fast voyages to India and summer cruises. Her winter cruises that year started with two short voyages to the Atlantic Islands, where she spent Christmas morning at anchor beneath the flowering slopes of Madeira. All this coincided with the start of political upheavals in Europe as British troops, which were part of an international force, marched through the French/German border town of Saarbrücken to oversee the forthcoming plebiscite. With Nazi swastikas and banners everywhere in the area the future looked ominous.

The *Viceroy of India* spent January and February of 1935 in the Eastern Mediterranean where her ports of call included Bizerta in Tunisia, Beirut, Haifa, Jaffa, Famagusta and Rhodes among others. There was sadness in Bizerta when one of the elderly passengers was found dead in a changing cubicle of the ship's swimming-pool. Once at sea again, there was excitement when a stowaway was discovered; a young Frenchman who had climbed up the mooring ropes at the quayside. He could not then be handed over to the civil authorities until the ship reached Port Said, where the passengers set out for tours to Cairo and to the Pyramids at Giza. The *Viceroy* returned to Tilbury on Saturday 23

The *Viceroy* spent the first two months of 1935 in the Mediterranean. In this view she is shown at Bizerta in Tunisia. *P&O*

On 22 June 1935 the *Viceroy* left Tilbury for a cruise to the North Cape and the Norwegian Fjords. This unusual photograph, taken at midnight on the night of 27/28 June by Second Electrical Officer Laurence (Sandy) Sanderson with his Brownie Box camera, shows the *Viceroy* at anchor off the North Cape.   *Laurence Sanderson*

The *Viceroy* off Molde in Norway during her Fjords cruise.   *Laurence Sanderson*

February 1935 and remained alongside her berth for a week, before sailing to Bombay.

On Friday 1 March 1935, the day before the *Viceroy* left London, a young man, Laurence (Sandy) Sanderson joined the vessel as Second Electrical Officer. He had served in the *Ranchi*, *Ranpura* and the *Maloja*, but the *Viceroy* was to be his favourite ship and, of course, being a turbo-electric ship she was an 'electrician's dream'. This is how he recalls those days: 'I served in this wonderful ship as one of the electrical officers on the fast Bombay run, where we were competing with the German liner *Potsdam*. We also cruised to the Northern Capitals, the Arctic Circle, the Mediterranean and the "one and only" East Indies Cruise, a wonderful experience. Some names come to mind after all these years, Captain E. J. Thornton (affectionately known as "Rastus"), the Chief Engineer, W. (Bill) Nimmo and Kenneth Cummins (the only deck officer I can remember). The *Viceroy* was a beautiful ship, both externally and internally and, propulsion-wise, I believe she was the mould for the French *Normandie*. I think the *Normandie's* Chief Engineer made a trip in the *Viceroy* to get the "feel" of a turbo-electric drive.'

After two voyages to Bombay and a cruise to Scandinavian waters in late June and early July, came the highlight of 1935 for Sandy Sanderson and all those aboard the *Viceroy*. That year marked the 25th anniversary of King George V's accession to the throne and to mark the occasion there were a number of national events, one of which was a Royal Fleet Review off Spithead. It was the fifth time that the King had reviewed his fleet and, sadly, it was to be his last for he died in January 1936. The *Viceroy of India* was one of a handful of passenger liners which were chosen to represent the merchant service at the Review, and the *Viceroy's* presence was incorporated into a short, but very special cruise. She completed her Fjords cruise at 2pm on Friday 5 July 1935, when she berthed alongside 105 berth in Southampton's Western Docks, and eight days later, on Saturday 13 July, she embarked her first class passengers for the 'special' cruise. She then sailed across the Channel to Le Havre. Sandy Sanderson takes up the story: 'We sailed with passengers from Southampton to Le Havre so as to legally break the customs bond and the bars could open. As we were leaving Le Havre we had a splendid view of the *Normandie*, which was arriving at the port from America.' After an overnight voyage back to the Solent, the *Viceroy* went to her anchorage at Spithead, arriving at 5.35am on Tuesday 16 July. Her position was in line K midway between Wootton Creek on the Isle of Wight and Gilkicker Point at Gosport, where she was the third ship in the line between the Union Castle ship *Warwick Castle* and Royal Mail's *Atlantis*. Other notable passenger liners which were present included the *Berengaria*, *Lancastria*, *Alcantara* and the *Arandora Star*. The actual review took place that same day when King George V and Queen Mary left Portsmouth Harbour on board the Royal Yacht *Victoria & Albert*, and accompanied by the Admiralty vessel *Enchantress*, made their way to the vicinity off the Spit Sand Fort where they received the Board of Admiralty and Flag Officers. The Royal Yacht then steamed back and forth between the lines of ships which had gathered at Spithead. There were over 160 warships assembled that day, including the battleships *Barham*, *Queen Elizabeth*, *Ramillies*, *Revenge*, *Rodney* and *Nelson*, together with the magnificent battle-cruiser *Hood*. There were aircraft-carriers, cruisers,

An excellent view of the *Viceroy* at anchor off Andalsnes in Romsdalsfjord on 1 July 1935.   *Laurence Sanderson*

Passengers playing deck tennis during the 1935 Fjords cruise. Note the additional motor launch which was carried by the *Viceroy* only when cruising. *Laurence Sanderson*

On 16 July 1935 the *Viceroy* took part in the Royal Fleet Review at Spithead. In this photograph passengers on the first class Sports Deck watch the Royal Yacht *Victoria & Albert* passing through the lines of assembled warships. *Laurence Sanderson*

and every other type of warship from the Home and Mediterranean Fleets. As Sandy Sanderson recalls: 'We had a grandstand view of the whole proceedings as the *Victoria & Albert*, with the "royals" aboard, steamed slowly up between lines D and E, then back down between F and G lines. That evening there was a firework display and on the next morning, headed by the Royal Yacht, the fleet sailed out to sea. After the fleet sailed we all gradually dispersed and went our separate ways—it was all very thrilling.'

At noon on Wednesday 17 July the *Viceroy* weighed anchor and left Spithead to complete her cruise which took her to Lisbon, Madeira and Corunna, before returning to Tilbury on 26 July. The next day she left the port once again, this time for a cruise in northern waters visiting Oslo, Copenhagen, Visby—the ancient capital of Gotland—then Stockholm and Hamburg At the end of that cruise on the morning of 9 August, the ship's company worked hard as usual to prepare for the next day when the *Viceroy* would sail from Tilbury on a Mediterranean cruise lasting almost a month. Her first ports of call were Gibraltar and Malta, and then she steamed out to the Eastern Mediterranean and Port Said where she disembarked those passengers travelling to view the Pyramids. She then headed north to Jaffa and Beirut, before returning to Port Said to collect the sightseers who had spent two days in Egypt. The cruise then continued north-west to Greece and west to the North African coast, arriving at Algiers on 1 September 1935. Here, probably few people on board paid much attention to the 16,484 gross

ton White Star liner *Doric*, which was also in the port. The *Doric* had left London on Monday 24 August for a two-week cruise and she had put in to Lisbon and Barcelona before calling at the North African port. After leaving Algiers both the *Doric* and the *Viceroy of India* were homeward-bound with the White Star vessel calling at Gibraltar on 3 September while the *Viceroy* arrived in Lisbon on the same day. Also at Lisbon that day was the brand new Orient liner *Orion*, which was returning to London after her 19-day maiden cruise to the Mediterranean. The *Viceroy* sailed during the evening of 4 September, at which time the *Doric* was steaming north off the Portuguese coast. At just after 3am on Saturday 5 September 1935, in a position Lat 41°-19′N/Long 9°-34′W, she encountered thick fog which at that time of year is prevalent in the area. At about 3.18am the *Doric*'s passengers were suddenly shaken by the impact of a collision as the bows of the small French steamer *Formigny* ploughed into the starboard side of the White Star liner, abreast No 3 hold. One of the *Doric*'s passengers recalled that he had been woken by a loud crash, followed by a grinding noise: 'The *Doric* lurched to starboard and I thought we had struck a rock. The stewards came round and told us to put on our life-jackets and get to boat stations.' Although there were no injuries, the force of the collision gouged a hole of some 14 feet by 6 feet, affecting an area from E Deck down to the Orlop Deck, between frames 59 and 63. No 3 hold was immediately flooded and further damage was caused on A and B Decks where the windlass

The *Viceroy* left Spithead, following the Fleet Review, on 17 July 1935. Here she is shown shortly before she left the Solent for Lisbon and Madeira. The Union Castle liner *Warwick Castle* is in the background. *Maritime Photo Library*

pipes were crushed. As the water gushed into No 3 hold, the vessel took on a list to starboard and, although she was not in any immediate danger of sinking, she was down by the head. SOS signals were sent out and these were received by the *Viceroy of India* and the *Orion* which both set course for the stricken *Doric* although, with thick fog blanketing the whole area, there could be no 'rescue dash'. There had always been some good-natured rivalry between P&O and Orient Line employees about which vessel arrived on the scene first, but according to Lloyd's records it was the *Viceroy of India* and this is confirmed by Sandy Sanderson who took photographs of the *Doric*. He clearly remembers that, upon their arrival, there were no other ships present— the *Formigny* literally having just carried on with her voyage. The *Viceroy* actually reached the *Doric* at 5.30am, just over two hours after the collision, and she immediately began to transfer the White Star liner's passengers. The *Orion*, which had left Lisbon at 5pm the previous day, arrived at the scene an hour later at 6.30am and between them the *Viceroy* and the *Orion* rescued all the *Doric's* passengers. By 9.30am the *Viceroy* had taken aboard 240 of them, together with the *Doric's* Assistant Cruise Director, while the *Orion* took another 475 passengers and a number of the *Doric's* crew members.

The *Doric* was able to set off for Lisbon under her own steam and she arrived there at 7pm that evening. Meanwhile the two other liners continued their voyage to Tilbury and

In late July and early August 1935 the *Viceroy* made a cruise to Europe's Northern Capitals. Here she is shown on 1 August 1935, framed by an archway of the old walls of Visby, the capital of Gotland. *Laurence Sanderson*

The *Viceroy of India* at anchor in the Thames looking very smart.

P&O

at noon that day an emotional thanksgiving service was held on *Viceroy's* second class Sports Deck. It was conducted by the Rev R. H. W. Kneese, Chaplain of Framlingham College, and was attended by all the rescued passengers as well as many of the *Viceroy's*. Both the *Viceroy of India* and *Orion* arrived back in the Thames on 7 September, with the *Viceroy* tying up at the Landing Stage at 10.15am that day. After disembarking all her passengers, the *Viceroy* went into the Tilbury dry dock for her annual overhaul, following which she went alongside No 33 shed in the docks. She was still alongside on 18 September when the *Doric* entered an adjoining berth, having undergone temporary repairs at Lisbon. It was thought that after discharging all her passengers' baggage she would go for more permanent repairs, but in the event the White Star Line decided that the cost was too great, and on 9 November 1935, the same day that the *Viceroy of India* sailed from London for Bombay, the *Doric* arrived at Newport in South Wales to be broken up. The dismantling process provided a year's work for 250 local men.

As the *Viceroy* steamed east once more, there were new political tensions in evidence, for the Italian army had invaded Abyssinia, and the League of Nations had voted to impose economic sanctions against Italy. For a time it seemed that Britain and France might intervene militarily, and so the strain was being felt particularly in the Red Sea region and around the colony of Aden. The political situation in Europe would continue to deteriorate, but for the time being the ships of the P&O were unaffected.

On 5 September 1935, towards the end of a three-week Mediterranean cruise, the *Viceroy* went to the aid of the White Star liner *Doric* which had been in collision. This photograph was taken soon after the *Viceroy* arrived on the scene on what was a very misty morning. The *Doric* is down by the head and the *Viceroy's* boats are alongside her.   *Laurence Sanderson*

Chapter Eight

The East Indies

Because of the war between Italy and Abyssinia, some shipping lines stopped using the Suez Canal and sailed to the east via Cape Town instead, one of these companies being the Blue Funnel Line. However, because of the stringent timetables demanded by the government mail contract, P&O continued to use the route via the Mediterranean and Suez, and in December 1935 the *Viceroy of India* made one of her most unusual voyages. She had arrived back in Tilbury after an 'express' run from Bombay at 7.30am on Friday 20 December 1935, in time for Christmas, and eight days later she left the port for her memorable journey. The first part of the voyage was, as usual, to Bombay, carrying both first and second class passengers, but it was not, however, to be one of her 'express' sailings.

and his manager, George Hawkins, joining the ship. He also recalls with affection the approachability of the world-famous author, in contrast to the 'stuffiness' of many of the first class passengers.

After leaving Marseilles in the early hours of 4 January 1936, the *Viceroy* called next at Malta, which was, in view of the Italian-Abyssinian War, heavily garrisoned with British troops and on alert for any possible aggression from nearby Italian bases in Sicily. Consequently Malta's famous Grand Harbour was well defended with anti-submarine nets and heavy guns. The *Viceroy* arrived off the harbour in the early evening of Sunday 5 January, with gusty winds blowing and daylight rapidly fading. The story can be taken up by Sandy Sanderson: 'It was late afternoon in the winter-time. The weather was boisterous, very windy with a rough sea, and

The *Viceroy* leaves Marseilles during one of her voyages east to Bombay.

P&O

Among the first class passengers there were a good many titled people, as readers of *The Times* were informed on sailing day. Nowadays it would be unthinkable to announce a prolonged absence from one's home but in pre-war days it was the 'done thing'. On this occasion readers learned that: 'Sir Daniel Cooper is leaving England today for the East Indies and expects to return on 9 March 1936.' Also, 'Lord and Lady Moynihan are sailing today in the liner *Viceroy of India* for the East Indies and will return on 9 March.' And, 'Major Sir Ralph and the Hon Lady Glyn are leaving England in the liner *Viceroy of India*.' These are but a few of the notices which appeared in that distinguished newspaper.

After calling at Gibraltar on New Year's Day, the *Viceroy* arrived in Marseilles three days later, where the 'overland' passengers embarked. It was here that Sandy Sanderson recalls the well-known American novelist Louis Bromfield,

Viceroy was about to enter Malta's Grand Harbour, between two moles or breakwaters. Due to the Italian-Abyssinian War there was also a defence boom across the harbour entrance, and in addition to the boom there was also a large gun, manned by the army, on the port side breakwater.

At the time I was the Duty Electrical Engineer in the engine-room and I was writing the log. The usual moves were requested in order to reduce speed, then there was a long pause. Suddenly the telegraph began to ring with a series of quick requests for "astern", "ahead", then "stop", followed by a heavy thump to the port side by the boiler-room which dislodged some spare parts that had been stored on bulkhead shelves. There was another, longer pause, after which we moved into the harbour and tied up to a buoy. I learned afterwards that the defence boom was opened to allow our entry to the harbour and Captain Thornton, who had been led to understand that the Harbour Pilot would board the ship inside the breakwater, started to move the ship between the moles. However, as the ship was moving ahead, the pilot boat appeared and the *Viceroy* had to go "full-astern" to avoid ramming it. At that moment, with the reduced speed, the *Viceroy* was caught by a very strong gust of wind from the starboard side and, with her very high superstructure, she was forced sideways onto the port side breakwater and the strong winds held her there for what seemed an age. I did hear that the army gun crew fled their posts as they saw the huge hull of the *Viceroy* bearing down on them.

I'm not sure how we eventually freed ourselves, but whilst the ship was pinned against the rocks it was impossible to use the main engines, in case the propellers were damaged on the rocks. Anyway we eventually entered the harbour.'

In the cooks' quarters of the ship some of the off-duty men and the butcher were playing bridge as the liner threaded her way through the 'S' turn of the nets and buoys of the island's defences when, suddenly, the shell plating on the outside of their cabin buckled with an almighty crash. The wooden panelling of the outer bulkhead splintered and their card-table crashed to the deck, scattering the cards around the room. The four players dived for the door, as it appeared that the vessel would be holed and the cabin flooded. Fortunately the mishap did not interfere with the voyage and once she was safely moored in the harbour an examination of the damage was carried out by officers from HM Dockyard. Although the plates of the ship's hull were buckled abreast the boiler-room, and a few feet above the water-line, it was clear that the damage could be temporarily put right whilst at sea and permanent repairs could be completed at the end of the voyage. As there was nothing which impaired the vessel's seaworthiness she was able to continue her journey east.

On 8 January 1936, the *Viceroy* arrived at Port Said for her southbound transit of the Suez Canal. Sandy Sanderson still has very vivid memories of the Italian troopships loaded with soldiers bound for the Abyssinian front, and the stark contrast of the hospital ships which were making their voyages back to Italy filled with pale, wounded and sick soldiers. It seemed to cast an all-pervading gloom over the *Viceroy* but, fortunately, once past Aden and with the ship finding the cooler breezes of the Arabian Sea, this feeling

A notable passenger on the 'East Indies' cruise was the American novelist Louis Bromfield. Here he is shown on fancy dress night (wearing Sandy Sanderson's white mess-jacket and sandals), with his manager, George Hawkins, and two elderly passengers. The photograph, which was autographed by Louis Bromfield, was taken in front of the mantelpiece in the first class Music Room. The portrait of Miss Elsie Mackay can be seen on the mantelpiece.

Laurence Sanderson

lifted and the happier atmosphere of former times returned.

The first leg of the journey ended at 1pm on Thursday 16 January 1936 when the great liner tied up alongside Bombay's Ballard Pier, where she was to remain for just over 48 hours. The next 29-day section of the *Viceroy's* voyage was to be a 'one-off' cruise, starting and finishing at Bombay, and for first class passengers only. The itinerary was Cochin, Colombo, Penang, Singapore, then via the coast of North Borneo to Macassar on Celebes Island (now Ujung Pandang on the Indonesian island of Sulawesi), Bali, Semarang, across the Java Sea and northbound this time up the Strait of Malacca to Belawan in Sumatra. From there the *Viceroy* headed west across the Bay of Bengal to Madras, then Colombo and finally back to Bombay. Fares for the cruise ranged from £32 to £50, with shore excursions being arranged by Thomas Cook & Sons Ltd. One of the highlights of the cruise was the chance to 'See the World's Famous Krakatau Volcano.'

Among the celebrities who embarked at Bombay were the Maharaja and Maharanee of Mysore, H. E. the Jehang of Bavada, the Raja and Ranee of Jamkhandi—the Indian state south-east of Bombay—and Sir Amberson and Lady Marten, Sir Amberson Marten having just retired as Bombay's Chief Justice. However, for Sandy Sanderson and some of the other officers, there was only one celebrity, and that was the American author Louis Bromfield who, with his friendliness and great sense of fun was a firm favourite.

The *Viceroy* left Ballard Pier at 7pm on Saturday 18 January and, as Sandy Sanderson recalls, 'We arrived at Colombo on the 21 January, the day after King George V had died, and I remember an RN sloop firing a 101-gun salute. We officers had to wear black armbands for a month.' Sandy also remembers that he and the Purser, Mr Harrington, were invited to a cocktail party organized by Louis Bromfield in the Maharaja of Mysore's suite. For Sandy the highlight of the cruise was the 'Crossing the Line' ceremony, which was a very elaborate affair spread over two days, and which he describes here: 'The ceremony took place in the Strait of Macassar between Borneo and Celebes. I took the part of the "barber", and it was a noteworthy performance which put me in mind of a Roman play. Perhaps it was because this was a special cruise that the ceremony was performed in an orderly and civilized manner with an understandable story-line which, I feel, was enjoyed by all. Both captains took part in the presentation

King Neptune's 'Court' assembled on *Viceroy's* after Sports Deck. Sandy Sanderson, who was the 'barber' is in the back row wearing the cut-down bowler hat.

Laurence Sanderson

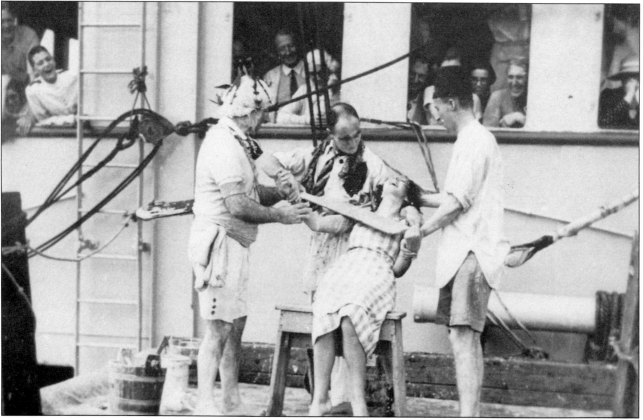

A 'reluctant' volunteer is shaved by the 'barber' before being ducked, much to the amusement of other passengers.

Laurence Sanderson

Author Louis Bromfield about to be thrown in as he is initiated into King Neptune's domain. *Laurence Sanderson*

With the ceremony over, Captain Thornton (with his back to the camera), is presented with the 'Order of the Royal Kipper' by King Neptune.
Laurence Sanderson

and the final bow, but it all started at about 9.30pm on Thursday 30 January, when King Neptune and his Queen ''boarded'' the ship on the forecastle. I can recall him loudly hailing the bridge and requesting permission to come on board. Captain Thornton answered in nautical style, whereupon the ''King'' demanded to know the name of the ship, the company and our destination. Captain Thornton gave him this information and then bade him and his ''Queen'' welcome, then a searchlight was switched on to illuminate the forecastle and the ''Royal Couple''. It was very dramatic and the passengers, who had gathered at the forward end of the Boat Deck and A Deck, loved it. After the introduction, the ''Royal Couple'' proceeded to the after Sports Deck where, complete with the ''Royal Court'', all the participants, who were fully dressed according to rank, were introduced to Captain Thornton. Finally that evening the ''King'' ordered everyone to appear before his court again at 2.30pm the next day and he then ''retired to the deep'' for the night.

Part two of the proceedings started on time the next day, which was Friday 31 January, when everyone took up their respective positions on the fore part of B Deck, just forward of the bridge where a makeshift wood and canvas pool had been rigged. The ''court'' was opened by the ''clerk'' and then the ''judge'' took over and gave instructions to the ''policemen'' to round up a list of ''criminals'' (who were volunteers from the passengers, among them a number of dignitaries, including Louis Bromfield), and bring them before the court for judgement and punishment. It was all very frivolous and amusing and it was quite a chase with some of the ''criminals'' hiding. As the ceremony proceeded and the victims were shaved and ducked, the platform round the pool got slippery with soap and I, together with my assistants, kept slipping into the pool where we too were ducked by the ''bears''. At the end of the afternoon the ceremony was closed and Captain Thornton was presented with the ''Order of the Royal Kipper'', and after he had thanked everyone, the proceedings closed with three hearty cheers. It was all very good fun and it was the sole topic of conversation on board for some days.'

Towards the end of the cruise, at Madras, Sandy was invited to a grand party which was hosted by Louis Bromfield at one of the city's top hotels, and four days later, on Sunday 16 February 1936, the cruise ended when the *Viceroy of India* berthed in Bombay's Alexandra Dock. Many of the passengers, including Louis Bromfield, and Lord and Lady Moynihan, were returning with the *Viceroy* via Marseilles to London, but they had to disembark for the six days that she was in the port loading mail and cargo. She left Bombay on 22 February and followed her normal mail route home to England, arriving in Tilbury on Monday 9 March 1936. The happy memories of the East Indies cruise were soon forgotten, for the headlines in *The Times* that day read: 'Herr Hitler brought off another of his audacious coups yesterday by denouncing the Rhine Treaty of Locarno and sending troops into the Rhineland.' The treaty, which had been signed in 1925, held Germany as an equal in the agreement to keep the Rhineland demilitarized, and was said to have marked the real end of the First World War. Its repudiation 11 years later signalled the prelude to the Second World War.

On her return to Tilbury on 9 March 1936, the *Viceroy* went into dry dock for repairs to her hull, following the damage sustained when she collided with the breakwater at the entrance to Malta's Grand Harbour. *Laurence Sanderson*

Chapter Nine

The Last Years Of Peace

Upon her arrival in London from the East Indies cruise, the *Viceroy* went into dry dock at Tilbury for both her annual overhaul and for repairs to her shell plating which had been damaged in the incident at Malta. She then made another routine voyage to Bombay, this time commanded by Captain E. A. J. W. Carter. She arrived back in London during the third week of April and sailed once again for India five days later, on 25 April 1936. Two days out to sea, at 1.30am on 27 April, whilst passing Cape Torinana in very heavy seas, she received an SOS message from the 3,500-ton British cargo vessel *SS St Quentin,* which was in distress off Ushant. The message read: 'Steering gear damaged, radio room flooded, in distress, require assistance' and despite the distance to be covered, Captain Carter altered course to go to her aid. However, in the severe storm which was raging, the *Viceroy's* speed was reduced to 16 knots and it was clear that she would take most of the day to reach the *St Quentin,* which was bound from South Wales to Newfoundland with a cargo of coal. In the heavy seas her cargo had shifted, causing her to develop a dangerous list and then, to add to her troubles, the steering gear had failed. Fortunately, Captain Carter soon realized that a number of other ships would be in the vicinity long before the *Viceroy* and he was able to continue his voyage to the first port of call, Tangier.

That summer the *Viceroy* made six cruises, the first four of which were to the Northern Capitals and the Fjords, calling at Gothenburg, Stockholm, Danzig and Copenhagen. The next cruise took her to Bordeaux, Lisbon and Madeira, and her final one was a three-week sojourn in the Mediterranean, with fares starting at 36 guineas (£37.80). However, by the end of September she was once again on the Indian mail service. She left London for her final sailing to India in 1936 at 4.05pm on 7 November, and at 6.45pm the next day she received an SOS call from the 4,400-ton German cargo vessel *SS Isis,* which had foundered off Land's End in a raging storm. However, at that time the *Viceroy* was 250 miles away in the Bay of Biscay, and as the two Cunarders *Queen Mary* and *Ausonia* were much nearer and had signalled that they were making for the stricken ship, Captain Carter did not consider it necessary to interrupt the *Viceroy's* voyage.

In the spring of 1937, P&O made arrangements for additional voyages from India to cater for a substantial number of extra passengers who were expected to attend the coronation of King George VI, which was set for 12 May that year. The *Viceroy of India* set out from London on one such voyage on 13 March 1937, and she was due to arrive back in Tilbury on 19 April with a large group of dignitaries who were attending both the coronation and the preceding

In the summer of 1936 the *Viceroy* made six cruises, one of which was to the Northern Capitals. Here she is shown at Stockholm. On the left is the Polish liner *MV Pilsudski,* which had entered service the previous year. *Andres Hernandez Collection*

The *Viceroy* at anchor in a Norwegian Fjord during one of her Scandinavian cruises.

P&O

festivities. The liner left Bombay for the homeward journey on 3 April 1937, fully booked with 700 passengers on board, and all went well for the first week. She arrived at Suez in the early hours of 10 April and as soon as the northbound convoy was ready, the *Viceroy* led the way along the narrow waterway towards Port Said. Although there were high winds and rain squalls in the area between Port Said and Ismailia, occasionally reaching hurricane force, there was nothing too unusual about the transit. The vessel was in the charge of a French pilot of the Suez Canal Company when, at 8.09am, at kilometre 154, there was a sudden fierce gust of wind from westward which caught the ship's high superstructure. She took a sharp sheer towards the west bank where her bow grounded, while the wind and tide forced the stern onto the east bank. The *Viceroy of India* was now firmly wedged right across the canal, blocking it completely. At 9.12am, just over an hour after she had grounded, and with the assistance of the Suez Canal Company's tug *Hercule*, the *Viceroy* was refloated and made fast to the east bank whilst wells were sounded and checks made to see if any damage had been caused. At 11.28am it was ascertained that the ship had not suffered any serious damage and Captain Carter, in company with a new pilot, was able to get her under way once again. However, the *Viceroy* was still some 65 miles from Port Said and, although the storms were abating, there were still high winds and rainstorms to contend with.

Some 40 minutes after she had got under way and despite the fact that the tug had been made fast ahead in order to

assist steering, at 12.08pm the *Viceroy* was again caught by a sudden squall, and again the bow took a sharp sheer in to the canal's west bank where she grounded once more. Five minutes later her stern was forced onto the east bank as before, but this time she was well and truly stuck, with the accompanying tug unable to move her. Once again Captain Carter ordered all wells to be sounded and, fortunately, the results were favourable with no leaks reported. However, it was thought that the rudder had been damaged and this was soon confirmed by a Suez Canal Company diver.

This time barges were brought alongside and work began to unload cargo from both forward and after cargo holds. That evening, at 9.13pm, the *Viceroy* was finally hove off the bank and refloated, with the help of tugs, both forward and aft. Because of her damaged rudder, she needed to undergo a full survey and so was made fast to the canal's west bank for this to be carried out. It was obvious the *Viceroy's* high superstructure had caused the problem for directly behind her in the convoy was the Orient Line's 20,000-ton passenger vessel *Orontes*, which had not been unduly inconvenienced by the weather conditions. It was 5.32am on 11 April before the *Viceroy*, together with the rest of the convoy, was able to continue her northerly transit of the Suez Canal, this time with the assistance of two tugs.

Once she had docked at Port Said, divers were able to make a more thorough examination of the rudder. It was found that the entire lower half of the rudder plating was torn and set over by about six feet, and a temporary repair, which entailed burning off the distorted parts, was carried out.

During the summer of 1936 the *Viceroy* made a three-week cruise to the Mediterranean. In this view there is a good turn-out of passengers on the first class Sports Deck for 'greyhound racing'. *P&O*

At the conclusion of the racing event, passengers and crew members pose for a photograph. *P&O*

A very happy group of passengers pose for the photographer on the first class Sports Deck.   *P&O*

The ladies' tug of war team get ready to 'heave away'.   *P&O*

This publicity photograph of passengers in the first class swimming-pool illustrates the magnificence of this compartment down on G Deck. It was, in fact, the first purpose-built swimming-pool on board a P&O ship.
P&O

Once this had been completed, during the afternoon of 12 April, a certificate of seaworthiness was obtained and the *Viceroy* was able to leave for Marseilles.

The four-day crossing of the Mediterranean from Port Said to Marseilles was accompanied by a lot of vibration aft and there was further inconvenience for the passengers when the voyage was terminated at the latter port and they had to continue the journey to London by train. Fortunately P&O's Marseilles agents were extremely efficient and they managed to arrange extra transport, so there was only the minimum delay. In fact, the passengers who were already booked on the overland route arrived in London only 24 hours late, whilst those who should have made the sea passage got back earlier than scheduled. The *Viceroy* then needed dry docking and so she sailed for Malta on 17 April, arriving there two days later. After eight days in the port, and with her rudder repaired, she was able to sail for Marseilles to take her place again in P&O's Indian mail service. Her next voyage to Bombay commenced on 1 May 1937, in Marseilles, just like the *Razmak* during the 1920s.

On her return to Tilbury on the afternoon of Monday 31 May 1937, after having been away from the port since mid-March, she embarked upon her summer cruising season. She made only three cruises during that year, all of them to northern waters and visiting several capital cities. In those days July and August were the busiest months at the Tilbury Landing Stage. On Thursday 31 July, for instance, the *Arandora Star* embarked her passengers and sailed on a cruise, and was then followed in quick succession by the *Viceroy of India*, the *Lancastria*, the *Montclare* and the *Highland Monarch*, all of them fully booked for their various cruises and voyages.

1938 was the *Viceroy's* last full year of service with the P&O Company, employed on both the mail run and cruising. During the first five months of the year she made three 'express' voyages to and from Bombay, calling only at Gibraltar, Marseilles and Aden on the outward journey and Aden, Malta and Marseilles on the homeward leg. Once again her summer cruises took her northwards, but with the political tensions in Europe coming to a head, and increasing government requirements for berths to India, for both service and civilian personnel, by mid-August she was back on the Indian mail service. In September 1938, at the time of Munich when all Europe 'held its breath', the *Viceroy* was homeward-bound in the Mediterranean, and by the end of December that year she had completed two more round voyages. In the New Year of 1939, with the immediate danger of war in Europe having receded, the *Viceroy of India* was preparing for yet another unique winter cruise—a 46-day voyage to both South America and South Africa.

She sailed from London on 20 January 1939, a cold, grey Friday, bound for Bahia and Rio de Janeiro in Brazil. From South America she sailed eastwards and on Saturday 11 February was the first P&O ship ever to call at Tristan da Cunha. The island's headman was ceremoniously received on board by Captain S. H. French, who was surprised to see the chief wearing a blue uniform with P&O buttons. A number of gifts were left by the passengers and crew, including a sewing-machine, a record-player and a chest of tea. Four days later the *Viceroy* called at Cape Town, and as she continued her homeward leg she reached the island of St Helena where, with favourable weather conditions, the passengers were able to land at Jamestown. Once ashore they had the opportunity of visiting the Briars Pavilion Museum and Longwood Old House, Napoleon's main residences during his exile there. Finally after calling at Freetown and Las Palmas, the *Viceroy* arrived back in Tilbury on Tuesday 7 March 1939. Four days later she left once again for Bombay, and made two round voyages to India before the end of May 1939. Ahead of her was a full season of summer cruises which should have taken her through to early October that year.

The *Viceroy* at anchor in the Thames during the late 1930s.

Alex Duncan

Chapter Ten

The *Viceroy* At War

The first cruise of the *Viceroy's* 1939 summer season was a two-week voyage to the Norwegian Fjords, commencing on 16 June. This was immediately followed on 1 July by a 16-day cruise to the Atlantic Isles, with an overnight stop at Madeira and calls at Las Palmas, Agadir and Lisbon. She arrived back at Tilbury on 17 July 1939 and spent the next 17 days there, undergoing her annual maintenance overhaul, during which time Germany continued to threaten the Polish state. She sailed again, on what was to be her final 'pleasure cruise', on Friday 4 August 1939, the day that Ribbentrop made the first overtures to the Soviet Ambassador in Berlin, which were eventually to lead to the Nazi-Soviet Pact and leave the way open for Hitler to invade Poland without the fear of a 'war on two fronts'. After leaving London she called at Leith and then headed into the Baltic, calling at Helsinki, Stockholm, Copenhagen and Oslo. The cruise had been due to end at Southampton on Friday 25 August but, on 23 August 1939, she was ordered back to London at full speed. It was the day that Molotov and Ribbentrop signed the Nazi-Soviet Non-Aggression Pact in Moscow, the implications of which were only too clear. The *Viceroy* arrived at Tilbury on Thursday 24 August and, as her passengers disembarked, cancellation notices were being sent out to everyone who had booked to sail on the liner's last two cruises of the season—a 13-day cruise to the Atlantic Isles on 26 August, followed by one to the Eastern Mediterranean for 23 days, both of which should have started from Southampton.

On the same day that the *Viceroy* arrived in Tilbury, a government telegram arrived at the P&O Head Office in London's Leadenhall Street. It read: 'Your vessel *Rawalpindi* is hereby requisitioned for government service.' It was the first of many such telegrams as over 60 medium-sized, fast passenger liners were taken over for conversion to armed merchant cruisers. The reliable P&O timetables were suddenly thrown awry as 12 of the ships were taken, one by one, off the trade routes and delivered into dockyard hands for the conversion work to begin. But there were still passengers to be carried and mails to be delivered, and on 29 August 1939 the company announced a complicated series of alterations to the sailing schedules as five ships which were, for the time being, unaffected by the requisitioning orders took on the duties that normally would have been carried out by 13 vessels. Part of the P&O announcement read: 'The *Viceroy of India* is taking the voyage of the *Rawalpindi* [26 August] from London to Shanghai.'

So, on the afternoon of Saturday 26 August 1939, as President Roosevelt sent personal cabled messages to Hitler in an attempt to avert war, and Britain and Poland signed a five-year mutual assistance agreement, which was an unambiguous declaration of Britain's intention to fight if Poland were to be invaded, the *Viceroy of India* left Tilbury Docks for the Far East. As she sailed, she passed the *Rawalpindi* which was being torn apart as she became one of the first armed merchant cruisers to be commissioned on the outbreak of the Second World War.

On 3 September 1939, the day that Britain declared war on Germany, the *Viceroy of India* was in the Mediterranean

An advertisement for part of P&O's 1939 summer cruising programme with the *Viceroy of India*. Only the first of these cruises was completed.   *Author's Collection*

VICEROY OF INDIA

AUG. 4

LONDON, FJORDS
NORTHERN CITIES
BALTIC, LONDON
21 DAYS • FARES FROM 36 GNS.

The Viceroy calls Leith outward and homeward to embark and disembark passengers. Leith to Leith 3 gns. less.

AUG. 26

SOUTHAMPTON
AZORES, LAS PALMAS
AGADIR, LISBON
SOUTHAMPTON
13 DAYS • FARES FROM 22 GNS.

SEPT. 9

SOUTHAMPTON
PALERMO, VENICE
DUBROVNIK
ALEXANDRIA, PORT
SAID, MALTA, LONDON
23 DAYS • FARES FROM 39 GNS.

P&O

FIRST CLASS
CRUISES

14 Cockspur St., S.W.I.   130 Leadenhall St., E.C.3.
Australia House, Strand, W.C.2, or local Agents.

just west of Malta and there was a certain amount of tension on board as it was not known how Italy would react to events. With a black-out in force on board, the atmosphere was subdued and very different from three weeks previously when she was still cruising in the Baltic. However, all went well and after calling at Alexandria and making a fast southbound transit of the Suez Canal, by 8 September she was in the Arabian Sea and the black-out was lifted. After Bombay her itinerary followed that of her East Indies cruise of 1935, with calls at Colombo, Penang and Singapore. From there she steamed north-east through the South China Sea to Hong Kong and on 30 September 1939 she made her first passage up the Whangpoo River and berthed alongside Shanghai's Old Ningpo Wharf.

After a ten-day stop-over in the Chinese port, the *Viceroy* returned home via the same route and she anchored in Plymouth Sound on 24 November 1939, the day after the German battle-cruisers *Scharnhorst* and *Gneisenau* sank the *Rawalpindi* in the icy waters between Iceland and the Faroes. By now the Admiralty were responsible for the movement of all shipping, and the *Viceroy* spent three days anchored off Plymouth before she was ordered to Avonmouth to discharge her cargo. Once this had been completed she was sent to Falmouth, where she arrived on 7 December 1939 and remained for 15 days. It was almost as though no one knew what to do with the great ship. Then, three days before Christmas, she was sent to Southampton where, after spending Christmas Day at anchor off Spithead, she arrived on 26 December. Early in the New Year she was dispatched

on another passenger and cargo voyage to the Far East, this time to Hong Kong and once again she went via the Mediterranean and Suez. The *Viceroy* sailed alone and unescorted on these wartime passenger voyages, relying on her speed to outrun or outmanoeuvre any enemy submarines. But once into the Indian Ocean life on board could be more relaxed and the deck lights would go on again. After an uneventful round voyage she arrived back in Southampton on 19 March 1940.

She began her third wartime voyage, again to Hong Kong, on 13 April 1940 and, just as she had done in pre-war years, she made calls at Gibraltar, Marseilles, Malta and Port Said. It was to be her last voyage through the Mediterranean and she arrived in Hong Kong in mid-May that year, as German troops rapidly advanced through the Low Countries and into France.

On 19 May 1940, as the *Viceroy* left Hong Kong for her voyage home, the news from Europe was not good. General Paul von Kleist's panzers had reached the English Channel west of Abbeville in France, thereby cutting off all Allied forces to the north, and three days later Boulogne, Amiens and Arras were occupied by the Germans. Not only was disaster looming in France, but in the Mediterranean events took an ominous turn as Mussolini abandoned all pretence of neutrality by declaring that: 'Italy is and intends to remain allied with Germany and...Italy cannot remain absent at a moment in which the fate of Europe is at stake.' It was now clear that British merchant shipping would be unable to use the Mediterranean Sea freely. After calling at Colombo and

The ill-fated liner *Rawalpindi* at Tilbury undergoing conversion from luxury liner to armed merchant cruiser. The *Viceroy* took over the *Rawalpindi*'s 26 August 1939 sailing from London to Shanghai.

P&O

The *Viceroy of India* at Cape Town on 13 August 1940, where she disembarked passengers rescued from the liner *Ceramic*.
Author's Collection

Bombay the *Viceroy of India* steamed south-west for Mombasa, Durban and Cape Town, a port she had last visited during her long winter cruise of January 1939. She arrived in Plymouth Sound on 7 July 1940 as preparations were under way all along Britain's south coast to defend the shores against the expected German invasion. The next day she steamed north to Liverpool where the voyage terminated on 9 July.

When the *Viceroy* left Liverpool on 22 July 1940, it was her last voyage in which she would carry only fare-paying passengers. She was commanded by Captain E. A. W. J. Carter and, once again, her destination was Shanghai. With the threat of a German invasion of Britain, many parents who lived and worked in overseas colonies became worried about their children who were 'at home' in boarding-schools, and consequently many decided that they wanted their children with them. As a result there were a number of such youngsters on board for this voyage, and some of them now recall their memories of the *Viceroy of India* on her journey east.

Mrs Susan Whitley and Mrs Pippa Boyle, as Susan and Pippa Kennaway, travelled to Malaya to join their parents. This is how Mrs Whitley remembers their childhood voyage: 'In the spring of 1940 we had been evacuated with our school on the south coast to a large private house in Cornwall. There were other girls at the school with colonial backgrounds like us. After the fall of France I can remember the excitement mounting as one by one their trunks appeared in the dormitory, and being told by the headmistress that they were leaving immediately to go abroad. Those were anxious days

for everyone as invasion was a real threat. Then came our turn—our trunks appeared—what a ''thrill'' that was. We were removed from school in the middle of term and taken to Liverpool to join the *Viceroy of India* for the voyage to Malaya to join our parents. We travelled second class and on our own, but arrangements were made for us to be put in the care of someone travelling on the ship, but I cannot remember who it was or anything about it.

As we were going up the gangway my knees felt weak and a terrible feeling of nausea came over me, and this was hours before we sailed. There was a strong smell of ''ship''—tar or oil probably—mixed with oranges and engine smells and it hung over everything. Pippa and I explored the ship but I felt very ill and took to my bunk before we sailed, and I was there for about four days being very seasick. I think we must have been going through the Bay of Biscay then. The cabin steward brought pots of tea with evaporated milk, as there was no fresh milk on board, and this made me feel worse.

When I felt better I started to enjoy it all very much. It was all very exciting, we were going ''out east'' to a completely new and different life, and we were getting away from the tedious old routine of school terms and holidays. The life on board was just as my mother had described her many journeys to and fro in the 1920s and 30s. The ship was still painted in its P&O colours, not grey like ships were later in the war. We played deck games and did all the usual things, but my main memory of the voyage is the swimming-pool. It was a truly marvellous place and we spent most of our days in and out of there. The man in charge was very kind and helpful to us—it was a gem of a place—small but perfect—and I think there was a diving-board.

Although we were travelling second class we looked into the first class places and were glad we weren't there. We thought the second class was much more fun. Everything was so different and exciting—the huge old baths down the passage from our cabin were filled with sea-water by a bathroom steward and we used soap that didn't lather. We worked our way through the enormous menus for days, and cups of thin broth were put out in the lounge or on deck for elevenses. Later, when the weather became warmer there were slabs of ice-cream on plates. My sister and I would lie on the long deck-chairs eating these ice-creams, unable to believe our luck that we were having them every day, but by the end of the voyage they were no longer such a treat.

I always have a dim memory of stopping to pick up some people from another ship around this time. It caused a stir of interest among the passengers at the time, but they couldn't have been on board for long. After Cape Town the incident was behind us and life went on as usual.'

Mrs Pippa Boyle was 13 at the time and recalls: 'At Liverpool we boarded the liner *Viceroy of India* and, to a schoolgirl, it was all very exciting and the *Viceroy* was luxurious, even in the second class. Our second stop was Freetown where, over the side of the ship, I bartered my red school linen bag for a bunch of bananas. Shortly after this port of call the collision between the *Testbank* and *Ceramic* took place nearby and we went to their rescue. This involved taking many children on board, who were also evacuees from England, but going to Australia. We took them all to safety in Cape Town and the approach to the port was thrilling, all those sparkling lights after the dreary black-out in England. The swimming-pool on G Deck was not only for the first class passengers, and I spent most of my time there, being instructed by the able warden. The library too was excellent with all the latest books.'

Mrs Lesley Crawford, who was also a passenger on the same voyage recalls: 'My mother, two sisters and I travelled out to Penang in the *Viceroy of India*, and the contrast from a strict boarding-school, after the severe winter of 1939/40 and the additional burden of rationing and the black-out, was striking. I had a dear little single cabin with a porthole, an intriguing fold-up wash-basin and a comfortable bunk, it was a great thrill. Then there were the peculiar salt-water baths

The *Viceroy*, fitted out as a 'landing ship infantry' (LSI) lies at anchor in the Clyde in late October 1942.   *Imperial War Museum*

with a small tub of fresh water on a fitment across each bath, which was another novelty. We had to buy salt-water soap and—a great luxury—this was all prepared by the bathroom steward who then came to call you when it was ready.

Another joy was the lavish unrationed food and the attractive dining-room, and I seem to remember a very pleasant sitting-out area outside the dining-room where we sat to watch the world go by. The beautiful swimming-pool was greatly patronized by us all and it was so different from a canvas pool on the deck. I seem to remember blue-green tiles and pillars. I recall that I learned to dive whilst on board, taught by a member of the crew who was a sort of life-guard and instructor.'

Mrs Felicity Cardew was also a schoolgirl at the time, and she too has vivid memories of the embarkation and the journey: 'On arriving at Liverpool we boarded the ship just before the start of an air raid, and I remember standing on the deck watching bombs raining down on other parts of the docks. At that age you do not think of the danger and I was more excited at meeting my best friend from school, Avril Walker. The ship seemed like heaven to me, I had my own little inside cabin with a blower which circulated cool air, although this became progressively warmer as we reached the tropics. I also had a bunk-bed, a wardrobe, a dressing-table and a dear little wash-basin which folded up into the bulkhead.

Coming from Britain, where life had already become difficult, there seemed to be so much of everything. The ship's shop was crammed with goods and I was given a beautiful music box which played a lullaby when you picked it up. I also bought a *Viceroy of India* sailor doll.

There was some dispute as to whether, at 13, I was to be classed as an ''adult'', and I was very glad to be informed that I could attend ''grown-up'' meals, which meant changing for dinner—very grand. The food was incredible, so much of everything, and we were travelling second class, so it must have been even better in the first class.

As second class passengers we were not allowed to visit the first class section, but my beautiful 21-year-old sister was much sought after by the many young army officers who were travelling in the first class section and they used to come down to see her and often persuaded her to visit them,

The *Viceroy of India* (in the centre of the photograph) at sea as part of the North African invasion fleet. This must be one of the last views of her before she was torpedoed.
Imperial War Museum

A close-up view of the torpedo damage to *Viceroy's* port side. As can be clearly seen, the Boat Deck and A & B Decks were badly torn and rolled back, but no hole in the ship's side was visible above the water-line.   P&O

though this was not strictly permissible. The crew and officers of the P&O were forbidden from mixing with the passengers.

On the voyage down to Cape Town we took on board passengers from a maritime collision and I remember seeing them come on board. There was an incident with an Australian, who was being deported, and they had problems with him, before he was locked in the brig until he was landed at Cape Town. We children had a great time on board the ship. There was a beautiful indoor swimming-pool where we spent a lot of time, and I can remember listening to an orchestra which played on deck during the afternoons. I think it was in the first class section, but we could hear it. The ship was like an enormous luxury hotel and, to me, it was something new and more luxurious than anything I had ever known. Coming from wartime Britain, the sun, the sea and the huge meals, together with the visits to exciting ports made it all seem like magic to me.'

After leaving Liverpool on 22 July 1940, the *Viceroy* called at Gibraltar and Freetown, and just over eight days later she was involved in a rescue operation, which has already been mentioned in her passengers' recollections. The *Viceroy* was about 300 miles off the town of Port Nolloth in South Africa, when she received an SOS message at 2.50am on 11 August. The 18,000-ton White Star Line vessel SS *Ceramic* had been in collision with the 5,000-ton cargo steamer *Testbank,* and her message read: 'Lat 27°-15′S/Long 10°E, in collision,

badly holed, require assistance.' In fact the *Testbank's* bow had ploughed into the starboard side of the *Ceramic*, abaft No 1 hold, causing severe damage and flooding. The *Ceramic* had nearly 700 passengers on board, many of whom were children, and with the ship unable to steam ahead or tow from forward it was imperative that the passengers were disembarked safely. As the *Viceroy* was within an hour's steaming distance, she was soon on the scene and boats from both ships were used to transfer the *Ceramic's* passengers to the *Viceroy*. By daylight the *Viceroy* was able to continue her voyage to Cape Town where she arrived on 13 August. Fortunately the weather had been calm and there were no casualties from either of the damaged vessels. Tugs from the port managed to get the crippled White Star liner under tow, stern first, and she arrived safely at Walvis Bay on 16 August. However, both the *Ceramic* and the *Testbank* were lost later in the war.

After disembarking the *Ceramic's* passengers at Cape Town, the *Viceroy* sailed again on 14 August and steamed north to Mombasa and Bombay, before calling at Colombo and Penang and arriving in Singapore on 6 September 1940. From there she went on to Hong Kong and Shanghai and then returned home by the same route, arriving in the Clyde on 13 November 1940. During her five-day stay at Glasgow she was partially fitted out as a troop transport, which involved little more than the removal of some of her more luxurious fittings and painting her battleship-grey. On 18

November she left on a trooping voyage, via Cape Town, to Suez, returning to Liverpool on 19 February 1941. She was then taken into dockyard hands and fully fitted out as a troop transport. Over the next four weeks the second class cabin accommodation was torn out and replaced with messdecks for the troops. Sections of her navigating bridge were plated in, and the liner was armed with one 6-inch gun, a Bofors gun and 14 Oerlikon guns. She was also fitted with Marlin machine-guns and two 12-pounder guns, and it was a very different *Viceroy of India* which sailed from the Clyde, in a convoy which included the *Strathnaver* and the *Strathmore*, on 24 March 1941, carrying troops to Cape Town and Bombay. On the return passage she crossed the Atlantic and embarked West Indian servicemen at Trinidad. The voyage was completed at Glasgow on 26 July that year, and she was then taken into her builder's yard for a major overhaul and for further work on her troop accommodation. For five months she remained at Glasgow and, upon completion of the work in the New Year of 1942, she bore little resemblance to the pre-war luxury liner she had once been.

She left the Clyde, after this refit, on 11 January 1942 with troops for the Middle East and, as before, took the route via Cape Town. On the return journey the vessel had trouble with her main propulsion machinery and during her four-week stop-over in Liverpool repairs were made to one of the turbo-alternators. It was during this period that Captain Carter left the ship upon being relieved by Captain S. H. French. The *Viceroy* made one more trooping voyage to Suez, leaving Liverpool on 28 May and returning to the port on 4 September 1942, when she was again taken into dock for major alterations. This time a number of her lifeboats and their davits were removed and replaced with ten assault landing-craft, five on either side of the ship. The *Viceroy* was to take part in the Allied landings in North Africa which, in conjunction with a westward advance from El Alamein,

would trap and defeat the Axis armies which were commanded by General Rommel.

The landings, code-named Operation Torch, were to take place on the morning of 8 November 1942, with forces being put ashore at Oran, Algiers and Casablanca. The *Viceroy of India* was to carry troops to Algiers as part of the first, fast convoy, which also included three other P&O liners, *Strathnaver*, *Cathay* and the *Mooltan* as well as the purpose-built troopship *Ettrick*. In mid-October 1942 she steamed north to the Clyde where the convoy was beginning to assemble and the troops were preparing to embark.

This convoy, which contained some 20 large troopships, left the Clyde on 26 October 1942, with the *Strathnaver* leading the way at the head of one column and the *Viceroy of India* directly behind her. They took a very roundabout route, steaming first into mid-Atlantic before turning south in the direction of the Azores and eventually curving southeast for the Straits of Gibraltar, through which they passed safely during the night of 6/7 November. However, in the early hours of 7 November, a submarine torpedoed the US transport *Thomas G. Stone* and she was forced to drop out of the convoy. The remaining ships arrived off Algeria that same evening and the landings went off without much opposition. After the troops had disembarked, the *Viceroy* remained at Algiers until 6pm on 10 November, and after embarking 22 passengers she was ordered to proceed independently to the Clyde via Gibraltar.

Soon after leaving harbour darkness fell and Captain French heard the sound of aircraft overhead, but not being able to identify them, and not wishing to give away the ship's position, the gunners did not open fire. The night of 10/11 November was fine and clear, with a smooth sea and a full moon. For just over ten hours after leaving Algiers the *Viceroy* steamed at 18½ knots on a westerly course, at the same time carrying out a continuous series of zigzag manoeuvres (described in the Admiralty books as Zigzag No

The *Viceroy*, listing heavily to port, goes down by the stern.

P&O

12), in order to confuse submarines. At 4.28am GMT on 11 November 1942, when the *Viceroy* was in a position Lat 36°-26′N/Long 00°-25′W, 31 miles north of Oran, she unfortunately passed the German submarine *U 407* which was on the surface charging her batteries. For the submarine commander the *Viceroy* presented an easy target, and he fired one torpedo which struck the liner on the port side abaft the after end of the engine-room in the vicinity of the emergency diesel generators. This is how Captain French remembered the event: 'I understand from those on watch that it was a noisy explosion, there was no flash, but a huge column of water was thrown up to a considerable height. The ship shook violently, all the lights went out, and she rolled over 3½ degrees to port. The upper deck was badly torn and rolled back, but no split in the ship's side was visible above the water-line.'

Sadly, the explosion had claimed the lives of four crew members, all of whom were on watch in the engine-room at the time. Two of them were Engineer Officers, Third Engineer, Mr E. Goodson, and Assistant Engineer, Mr R. E. Bishop. The other two fatalities were Indian engine-room staff.

Captain French again takes up the story: 'The emergency dynamo was brought into action, an SSS message was sent out giving our position, and I ordered all boats to be turned out with the crew standing by. The engines were shattered, but I had great hopes of saving the ship if we could arrange to be towed. At daylight a small drifter or minesweeper came along and signalled "How long will you take to sink?" which

appeared to me to be rather premature; shortly afterwards a destroyer appeared and they too signalled to know if we were sinking. This was *HMS Boadicea*, and I replied that although the ship was sinking slowly, I thought there would be a chance to save her if they would take us in tow, first taking off most of the crew. This was agreed upon and while the destroyer carried out a submarine sweep, the men got into the boats and all six were successfully lowered. These boats accommodated 80 people and the six were just sufficient for the personnel on board. They boarded the *Boadicea*, whilst 40 of us remained in the *Viceroy of India* as a working party. We made tow lines fast, but the vessel was already 18 feet lower in the water, going down all the time by the stern and listing more heavily, and at 7am I decided to abandon ship. We held on a little longer, but she continued to sink and at 7.40am we left the ship and boarded *HMS Boadicea*. She stood by and we watched the vessel slowly sinking until she finally disappeared at 8.07am, going down by the stern.'

For the vessel's crew members, from Captain French downwards, it was a sad sight and particularly so for Ed Roffey, the Chief Steward, who had been with the ship since she first entered service, nearly 14 years previously.

The *Viceroy's* crew members were taken to Gibraltar in *HMS Boadicea* and they were landed there at 6pm that same day. From Gibraltar they were repatriated to the UK aboard the *Llangibby Castle*, after which they went their separate ways. It was a very sad end to what was, without doubt, one of the P&O Company's finest ships.

The final plunge! A very sad end to one of P&O's finest passenger ships. The *Viceroy of India* sinks by the stern at about 8.07am on 11 November 1942.

P&O

SS Viceroy of India

Principal Particulars

Length Overall:	612 ft
Length B.P:	585 ft
Breadth Moulded·	76 ft
Gross Tonnage:	19,648
Net Tonnage:	10,087
Cargo Capacity:	217,749 cu ft
Main Propulsion Machinery:	Twin propellers driven by Electric Motors, powered by two Turbo-Alternators: 17,000 SHP: Speed 18 knots:

Passengers:

First Class (In 415 rooms):	415
Second Class (In 100 rooms):	258
Crew:	420

Appendix Two

Honours 1942:

B.E.M.

E. Duvoisin	Chef
W. Murray	Carpenter
R. E. Handforth	Boatswain
J. Menzies	Pantryman

Acknowledgements

Special thanks to the following:

Mr Derek H. Deere, Editorial Director of Marine Publications International Ltd, Houndmills, Basingstoke, Hampshire, for permission to use photographs from the *Shipbuilder* magazine.

Mr Laurence (Sandy) Sanderson, West Ewell, Surrey, for his very vivid memories and the use of his photographic collection.

Mr Norman Pound, P&O Chief Engineer, for checking the text of Chapter Four and correcting any technical errors.

Mr Andres Hernandez, Miami, Florida, USA, for the loan of his photographic collection.

Thanks also to the following:
Mr Bob Aspinall, Librarian, Museum of London, PLA & Museum in Docklands Project: Mrs P. Boyle, Finchley, North London: Mrs F. Cardew, Woking, Surrey: Mr Ernest H. Cole, North Harrow, Middlesex: Mrs L. Crawford, Grayshott, Surrey: Mr Alex Duncan, Gravesend, Kent: Mr Paul Kemp, Dept of Photographs, Imperial War Museum, London: Mrs Lynn Palmer and Mr Stephen Rabson, P&O Group Information, London: Mr Adrian Vicary, Maritime Photo Library, Cromer, Norfolk: Mrs Susan Whitley, Haslemere, Surrey. Finally to my wife Freda and daughters Caroline & Louise.